Pygmalion Reconsidered

A Case Study in Statistical Inference: Reconsideration of the Rosenthal-Jacobson Data on Teacher Expectancy

Janet D. Elashoff

Stanford University

and

Richard E. Snow

Stanford University

Charles A. Jones Publishing Company
Worthington, Ohio

Contemporary Educational Issues
National Society for the Study of Education

Farewell to Schools??? Daniel U. Levine and Robert J. Havighurst, Editors

Models for Integrated Education, Daniel U. Levine, Editor

Accountability in Education, Leon M. Lessinger and Ralph W. Tyler, Editors

Pygmalion Reconsidered, Janet D. Elashoff and Richard E. Snow

Reactions to Silberman's CRISIS IN THE CLASSROOM, A. Harry Passow, Editor

1 2 3 4 5 6 7 8 9 10 / 76 75 74 73 72

Library of Congress Catalog Card Number: 74-184313
International Standard Book Number: 0-8396-0017-8

Printed in the United States of America

Series Foreword

Pygmalion Reconsidered is one of a group of five publications which constitute the first of a series published under the auspices of the National Society for the Study of Education. Other titles are:

Farewell to Schools??? edited by Daniel U. Levine and Robert J. Havighurst

Accountability in Education, edited by Leon M. Lessinger and Ralph W. Tyler

Reactions to Silberman's CRISIS IN THE CLASSROOM, edited by A. Harry Passow

Models for Integrated Education, edited by Daniel U. Levine

For more than seventy years the National Society has published a distinguished series of Yearbooks. Under an expanded publication program, beginning with the items referred to above, the Society plans to provide additional services to its members and to the profession generally. The plan is to publish each year a series of volumes in paperback form dealing with current issues of concern to educators. The volumes will undertake to present not only systematic analyses of the issues in question but also varying viewpoints with regard to them. In this manner the National Society expects regularly to supplement its program of Yearbook publication with timely material relating to crucial issues in education.

In addition to their extensive reanalysis of the data from the original Pygmalion study by Robert Rosenthal and Lenore Jacobson, the authors of *Pygmalion Reconsidered* offer a critique of that study, comments on design and measurement problems in educational research, and a chapter (by J. Philip Baker and Janet L. Crist) on replications and studies related to the *Pygmalion* experiment. In addition, the volume includes a response to the Elashoff and Snow report prepared by Professor Rosenthal in collaboration with Donald B. Rubin, with a final answer.

The National Society for the Study of Education wishes to acknowledge its appreciation to all who have had a part in the preparation of this book.

Kenneth J. Rehage
for the Committee on the Expanded Publication
Program of the National Society for the Study of
Education

Foreword

Like any scientist, the psychologist senses the plausibilities in his field. It is extremely implausible that infrahumans can learn to speak good English and less implausible that children can learn to solve differential equations.

How plausible are statements about intentional changes in human intelligence? Half a century of research has shown that such changes are hard to make. They have been claimed by persons using intensive treatments in preschools. They have been effected by profound alterations in the person's whole environment—alterations like moving out of a barren orphanage into an enriched middle-class home. But, even so, no one has yet been able to change IQ substantially in any controlled and consistent way. We cannot improve IQ as dependably as we can improve knowledge of mathematics or languages.

Psychologists and educators are still working on ways to improve intelligence. They are placing their bets on radical and intensive improvements of the "curriculum" and "teaching methods" in the home and school during infancy and childhood.

I had this kind of feeling for the plausibilities when I first encountered the work of Robert Rosenthal and Lenore Jacobson. I was serving as a discussant in the symposium at the American Psychological Association meetings in 1966 at which they reported their findings. It seemed implausible to me that the IQ, which had proven so refractory, would yield to the admittedly weak treatment administered to the teachers in their experiment. In my discussion, I said as much and also cited weaknesses in the design, measurement, and analysis aspects of their experiment.

A year later, I was asked to review the manuscript of *Pygmalion in the Classroom* for its publisher. Again I criticized the work roundly. Then the book appeared. As Professors Elashoff and Snow indicate, it received high praise from almost all reviewers. But most of the reviewers were untrained in psychological measurement and statistical analysis. Technically competent reviewers, like R. L. Thorndike and R. E. Snow, seriously questioned the validity of the Rosenthal-Jacobson data and conclusions. In his review, Snow promised a reanalysis of the data. This book contains that reanalysis, which he and Elashoff did together. It shows more thoroughly than ever the questionable nature of the Rosenthal-Jacobson data and methods.

Pygmalion in the Classroom got more attention in the mass media than any other product of the behavioral sciences in the 1960's. It struck a responsive chord among millions who were looking for an explanation of the educational problems of children from low-income areas—problems intimately connected with our most poignant national concerns. Now that the Rosenthal-Jacobson work has been thrown in doubt, one can only hope that the whole business will not—as I feared when reviewing the manuscript—undermine confidence in psychological research.

Do teachers' expectations affect things other than IQ—what teachers try to teach and thus what students learn, how students feel about themselves, how they get along with the teacher and their fellow students? Here affirmative answers seem highly plausible on the basis of much previous research. The task of psychologists and other behavioral scientists is to use valid methods to reveal such effects. Then, if these effects are undesirable, we should develop techniques to guard against them. The positive residue of the *Pygmalion* affair is renewed attention to the hypothesis that teachers' expectations make a difference in the classroom. Research workers are now taking a fresh look at these phenomena. This book also contains a review, by Philip Baker and Janet Crist, of this more recent work. For our present hard-won sophistication about the problem, all of us should be grateful to the authors of this powerful book.

N. L. Gage

Preface

Increasingly, investigators are attempting research on difficult human problems. Many students in education and the behavioral sciences are preparing for research careers; others are being called upon to read and use the results of research. They need to be confronted with the difficult problems in conducting research and in the analysis and criticism of research data.

Pygmalion Reconsidered is a detailed criticism and case history of a data analysis. At one level, it is a critical evaluation of a research report. At another level, it is a detailed account of technical issues important in evaluating research. At still another, it is a comparison of the merits of, and the results obtained from, alternate analytic approaches to the same data. It can serve as a special kind of supplement to courses on research methodology and statistical analysis for the student and the practicing researcher or educator.

This book is a case study of the research study *Pygmalion in the Classroom* by Rosenthal and Jacobson (1968) and the report of an extensive reanalysis of the Rosenthal and Jacobson data. The study was chosen for detailed examination for two reasons: First, it addresses a major social problem, has received nationwide attention, and has prompted a number of similar studies in the area; second, its basic design, measurement problems, and the statistical procedures used in its analysis and reanalysis are typical of those encountered frequently in educational or behavioral science research.

This book is a revised and expanded version of Technical Report No. 15, *A Case Study in Statistical Inference: Reconsideration of the Rosenthal-Jacobson Data on Teacher Expectancy,* by Janet Dixon Elashoff and Richard E. Snow, published

December 1970 by the Stanford Center for Research and Development in Teaching, School of Education, Stanford University.

Portions of the work described in that report were supported within a USOE-sponsored project on the nature of aptitude (OEC 4-6-061269-1217), and portions were supprted by the Stanford School of Education and the Stanford Center for Research and Development in Teaching under Contract No. OE-6-10-078. The opinions expressed in this publication do not necessarily reflect the position or policy of the Office of Education, and no official endorsement by the Office of Education should be inferred.

Dr. Rosenthal and Dr. Jacobson have cooperated in providing copies of their original data and permission to reanalyze them. We gratefully acknowledge their assistance. Portions of *Pygmalion in the Classroom: Teacher Expectation and Pupils' Intellectual Development,* by Robert Rosenthal and Lenore Jacobson, copyright © 1968 by Holt, Rinehart and Winston, Inc. are reprinted by permission of Holt, Rinehart and Winston, Inc. All of Rosenthal's and Jacobson's original data can be found in Elashoff's and Snow's original report upon which this book is based.

The authors wish to thank J. Philip Baker and Janet L. Crist for their chapter on replications and studies related to the *Pygmalion* experiment. N.L. Gage, L.J. Cronbach, and Ingram Olkin have given many helpful comments and criticisms during various stages of the work. The assistance of Bruce Bergland, John Burke, James Eusebio, Catherine Liu, Akimichi Omura, Donald Peters, and Trevor Whitford is gratefully acknowledged. Many others have offered helpful suggestions on the manuscript.

Special thanks go to Judy Turner, who put it all together.

Janet D. Elashoff
Richard E. Snow

Contents

Chapter

Appendices

I

Introduction

This book is a critical evaluation of the research study reported by Robert Rosenthal and Lenore Jacobson (1968b)* and the report of an extensive reanalysis of their data.

In his 1966 book, Rosenthal, a Harvard social psychologist, demonstrated the importance of experimenter effects in behavioral research, thereby developing a new field for psychological inquiry (Rosenthal, 1966). After a discussion of the experimenter as biased observer and interpreter of data, and of the effects of relatively permanent experimenter attributes on subjects' responses, a series of experiments was summarized purportedly showing the effects of experimenter expectancy in studies of both human and animal behavior. Many suggestions were offered on the control and reduction of self-fulfilling prophecies in psychological research. To suggest the generality and importance of such phenomena, the book closed with a preliminary analysis of data on teacher expectancy effects and pupil IQ gains in elementary school. Those closing pages (pp. 410-413) then were expanded by Rosenthal and Jacobson for journal presentation (1966, 1968a) and for wider circulation in book form (1968b). For brevity in the present report, we will refer to the original study, authors, and book source *Pygmalion in the Classroom* as RJ.

Our criticism and reanalysis is intended to serve several purposes. Its major aim is to provide a pedagogical aid for students, researchers, and users of research. Thus it offers an extensive critique of a study, its design, analysis, and reporting. This critique provides a vehicle for examining common methodological problems in educational and behavioral science research, and for discussing and comparing statistical methods which are widely used but seldom well understood. The reanalysis of the RJ data provides a demonstration of the wide variation in apparent results

---

*Information within parentheses refers to the References section at the end of the book.

when similar analytic procedures are applied to data with sampling and measurement problems. Finally, we sought to identify the conclusions that can reasonably be drawn about teacher expectancy from the RJ study, since the wide publicity attracted by the study's expectancy hypothesis may have already sensitized teachers to this type of experiment and thus prejudiced attempts at replication.

For pedagogical purposes, we have included criticisms ranging from major to relatively minor issues, from points of general information readily available to most educational researchers, to points buried in the statistics literature. It might be argued that our criticisms are unnecessarily stringent, that faults in the RJ study are common faults or that RJ use procedures consistent with "standard practice" in the field. Even if one feels that RJ should not themselves be unduly criticized for faults common in standard practice, one must begin somewhere to examine and improve standard practice. We can see no better place to begin than with a widely quoted popular book that is also ". . . intended for students of education and of the behavioral sciences, generally, and for research investigators in these fields." (RJ, p. viii)†

Summary of the RJ Study as Originally Reported

The original study involved classes designated as fast, medium, and slow in reading at each grade level from first through sixth in a single elementary school, "Oak" School in South San Francisco. During May 1964, while *S*s (children) were in Grades K through 5, the "Harvard Test of Inflected Acquisition" was administered as part of a "Harvard-NSF Validity Study." As described to teachers, the new instrument purported to identify "bloomers" who would probably experience an unusual forward spurt in academic and intellectual performance during the following year. Actually, the measure was Flanagan's *Tests of General Ability* (TOGA), chosen as a nonlanguage group intelligence test providing verbal and reasoning subscores as well as a total IQ. TOGA was judged appropriate for the study because it would probably be unfamiliar to the teachers and because it offered three forms, for Grades K-2, 2-4, and 4-6, all of similar style and content. As school began in Fall

†From *Pygmalion in the Classroom: Teacher Expectation and Pupils' Intellectual Development,* by Robert Rosenthal and Lenore Jacobson. Copyright © 1968 by Holt, Rinehart and Winston, Inc. Reprinted by permission of Holt, Rinehart and Winston, Inc. This credit line applies to all quotations from this source identified in the text by the initials RJ, a page reference, and the symbol (†).

1964, a randomly chosen 20% of the Ss were designated as "spurters." Each of the 18 teachers received a list of from one to nine names, identifying those spurters who would be in his class. TOGA was then readministered in January 1965, May 1965, and May 1966.

RJ chose to obtain simple gain scores from the pretest (May 1964) to the "basic" posttest, a third testing in May 1965, and to make their primary comparisons with these. The main statistical computations were analyses of variance. Factors used in the analyses were treatment group (experimental vs. control), grade (first through sixth), ability track (fast, medium, slow), sex, and minority group status (Mexican vs. non-Mexican). An analysis of variance of the full 2x6x3x2x2 classification was neither planned nor possible since the experimental group contained only 20% of the children, only 17% of the total were Mexican, and the experiment was not designed to ensure equal representation by sex and ability track. Thus, with only 382 children actually included in the experiment, many of the 144 cells of the complete cross-classification table were empty (see our Table 2 for classroom by treatment group cell sizes). RJ calculated several two-and three-way analyses of variance using the unweighted means approximation to deal with problems of unequal cell frequencies.

The main results for Total IQ gain from pretest to basic posttest are presented in Chapter 7 of the RJ book. The main table of data is their Table 7-1, reproduced here as Table 1, which shows mean gain in Total IQ for each grade and treatment group. "Expectancy advantage" was defined as mean gain for the experimental group minus mean gain for the corresponding control group (also called "excess of gain" by the experimental group). An excerpt from RJ's discussion follows:

The bottom row of Table 7-1 gives the over-all results for Oak School. In the year of the experiment, the undesignated control-group children gained over eight IQ points while the experimental-group children, the special children, gained over twelve. The difference in gains could be ascribed to chance about 2 in 100 times (F = 6.35).

The rest of Table 7-1 and Figure 7-1 show the gains by children of the two groups separately for each grade. We find increasing expectancy advantage as we go from the sixth to the first grade: the correlation between grade level and magnitude of expectancy advantage (r = −.86) was significant at the .03 level. (p. 74)†

The report continues with similar tables giving results for separate Reasoning and Verbal IQ scores and showing gain or "expectancy advantage" for breakdowns by sex and ability track. Brief profiles of a "magic dozen" of the experimental group children are

TABLE 1

Mean Gain in Total IQ After One Year by Experimental

and Control-Group Children in Each of Six Grades

(Reprinted from RJ, their table 7-1, p. 75)[†]

	Control		Experimental		Expectancy Advantage	
Grade	$\underline{N}$	Gain	$\underline{N}$	Gain	IQ Points	One-tail $p < .05$*
1	48	+12.0	7	+27.4	+15.4	.002
2	47	+ 7.0	12	+16.5	+ 9.5	.02
3	40	+ 5.0	14	+ 5.0	- 0.0	
4	49	+ 2.2	12	+ 5.6	+ 3.4	
5	26	+17.5(-)	9	+17.4(+)	- 0.0	
6	45	+10.7	11	+10.0	- 0.7	
Total	255	+8.42	65	+12.22	+ 3.80	.02

*Mean square within treatments within classrooms = 164.24

FIGURE 1: EXPECTANCY ADVANTAGE AFTER FOUR, EIGHT
AND TWENTY MONTHS AMONG UPPER AND LOWER
(TWO) GRADES (Asterisk indicates $p < .10$ two-tail).
(Reprinted from RJ, their figure 9-5, p. 141.)[†]

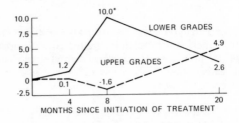

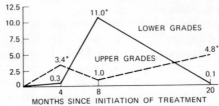

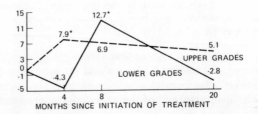

also included, detailing their pre- and posttest IQ scores, along with anecdotal descriptions of each child. The over-all results are interpreted as showing ". . . that teachers' favorable expectations can be responsible for gains in their pupil's IQs and, for the lower grades, that these gains can be quite dramatic." (p. 98)†

Also provided were supplemental analyses of data from the second and fourth TOGA administrations as well as graded achievement in various school subjects, teacher ratings of classroom behavior, and a substudy of general achievement test scores. Charts such as those reproduced in Figure 1 are given to illustrate "the process of blooming." They show excess of IQ gain by experimental group over control group across testing occasions for various breakdowns of the school population.

The book concludes with a discussion of selected methodological criticisms of the study and more general methodological aspects of Hawthorne and expectancy studies, including design suggestions. It also offers speculation on possible processes of intentional and unintentional influence between teachers and students, and closes as follows:

There are no experiments to show that a change in pupils' skin color will lead to improved intellectual performance. There is, however, the experiment described in this book to show that change in teacher expectation can lead to improved intellectual performance.

Nothing was done directly for the disadvantaged child at Oak School. There was no crash program to improve his reading ability, no special lesson plan, no extra time for tutoring, no trips to museums or art galleries. There was only the belief that the children bore watching, that they had intellectual competencies that would in due course be revealed. What was done in our program of educational change was done directly for the teacher, only indirectly for her pupils. Perhaps, then, it is the teacher to whom we should direct more of our research attention. If we could learn how she is able to effect dramatic improvement in her pupils' competence without formal changes in her teaching methods, then we could teach other teachers to do the same. If further research shows that it is possible to select teachers whose untrained interactional style does for most of her pupils what our teachers did for the special children, it may be possible to combine sophisticated teacher selection and placement with teacher training to optimize the learning of all pupils.

As teacher-training institutions begin to teach the possibility that teachers' expectations of their pupils' performance may serve as self-fulfilling prophecies, there may be a new expectancy created. The new expectancy may be that children can learn more than had been believed possible, an expectation held by many educational theorists, though for quite different reasons (for example, Bruner, 1960). The new expectancy, at the very least, will make it more difficult when they encounter the educationally disadvantaged for teachers to think, "Well, after all, what can you expect?" The man on the street may be permitted his opinions and prophecies of the unkempt children loitering in a dreary schoolyard. The teacher in the schoolroom may need to learn that those same prophecies within her may be fulfilled; she is no casual passerby. Perhaps Pygmalion in the classroom is more her role. (p. 182)†

Organization of the Book

At this point, we give the reader a preview of the contents of the rest of the book. We have arranged our comments in six major sections: review of the RJ report, discussions of design and sampling problems, measurement problems, summary of analysis and conclusions, replications of the RJ study, and analysis problems and reanalysis results in Appendix A.

The research report is a crucial part of the research process. Chapter II contains a critical review of *Pygmalion* as a research report and suggests that the report as a whole is inadequate. Descriptions of design, basic data, and analysis are incomplete. Inconsistencies between text and tables, overly dramatic conclusions, oversimplified, inaccurate or incorrect statistical discussions and analyses all contribute to a generally misleading impression of the study's results.

Chapter III examines RJ's experimental design and sampling procedures. The major difficulties discussed are the lack of clarity about the details of assignment to treatment groups, subject losses during the experiment, and the lack of balance in the design. These difficulties are especially important in the RJ study since the experimental group showed higher pretest scores on the average.

In Chapter IV, we examine the IQ scores actually obtained by children in Oak school, and questions of norming, reliability, and validity for these measurements. Histograms of the score distributions in each grade are shown. The number of IQ scores below 60 and above 160, especially for Verbal and Reasoning subscores, raises doubts about the validity of the experiment as a whole and the results of certain statistical techniques in particular.

Chapter V contains a brief overview of our reanalysis and overall conclusions about the results of the RJ study and concludes with some general methodological recommendations.

Chapter VI by Philip Baker and Janet Crist summarizes the results of attempted replications of the RJ study. Several of the magazine and journal reviews of *Pygmalion in the Classroom* are reprinted in Chapter VII.

Appendix A contains detailed discussions of the methodological problems involved in the analysis of a complex study, comments on RJ's choice of analysis, and the results of our reanalyses. We demonstrate the wide variation in apparent results obtained from slightly different statistical approaches when serious imbalance in the design and major measurement problems exist.

Appendix B contains a glossary of terms and procedures referred to in the text.

II

Pygmalion in the Classroom as a Report of Original Research

Before discussing methodological aspects of the RJ study, we consider it appropriate to examine the RJ book as a report of original research. A researcher's responsibility does not end when the experiment has been conducted and analyses concluded; he must report to the public his methods and findings. This is not a trivial final step but a crucial part of the research process. If the reader is misled about the results, it no longer matters how much care went into the performance of the experiment. A careful reading of the report should provide the reader with sufficient information to allow replication of the study, to allow replication of the data analyses if provided with the data, and to allow him to draw his own conclusions about the results. Stated conclusions, tables, and charts should be carefully presented so that the uninformed reader will not be misled. All studies have weaknesses in design, execution, measurement, or analysis. These should be carefully discussed in the report because they affect the interpretation of results.

Careful reporting is especially important when the report receives considerable attention from methodologically unsophisticated readers, as in the case of *Pygmalion*. The phenomenon of teacher expectancy might be of central importance in the improvement of education, particularly if the scholastic development of disadvantaged children were strongly dependent on such effects. The problem then is of considerable social moment and the results of the RJ work have been widely distributed with noticeable impact in the news media. The following represents a sample of popular reaction:

Can the child's performance in school be considered the result as much of what his teachers' attitudes are toward him as of his native intelligence or his attitude as a pupil? . . . *Pygmalion in the Classroom* is full of charts and graphs and statistics and percentages and carefully weighed statements, but there are conclusions that have great significance for this nation. . . . Among the children of the first and second grades, those tagged "bloomers" made astonishing gains. . . . TOGA's putative prophecy was fulfilled so conclusively that even hard-line social scientists were startled. (Coles, *The New Yorker,* April 9, 1969)

Here may lie the explanation of the effects of socio-economic status on schooling. Teachers of a higher socio-economic status expect pupils of a lower socio-economic status to fail. (Hutchins, *San Francisco Chronicle*, August 11, 1968)

Jose, a Mexican American boy . . . moved in a year from being classed as mentally retarded to above average. Another Mexican American child, Maria, moved . . . from "slow learner" to "gifted child,". . . . The implications of these results will upset many school people, yet these are hard facts. (Kohl, *The New York Review of Books*, September 12, 1968)

The findings raise some fundamental questions about teacher training. They also cast doubt on the wisdom of assigning children to classes according to presumed ability, which may only mire the lowest groups into self-confining ruts. (*Time*, September 20, 1968)

Other comments appeared in the *Saturday Review* (October 19, 1968), and a special issue of *The Urban Review* (September, 1968) was devoted solely to the topic of expectancy and contained a selection from *Pygmalion.* (Several of the reviews are reprinted in Chapter VII.) Rosenthal was even invited to discuss the results on NBC's "Today" show, thus reaching millions of viewers with the idea. The study was also cited in at least one city's decision to ban the use of IQ tests in primary grades:

The Board of Education's unanimous action was founded largely on recent findings which show that in many cases the classroom performance of children is based on the expectations of teachers.

In one study conducted by Robert Rosenthal of Harvard University, the test results given to teachers were rigged, but the children performed just as teachers had been led to expect based on the IQ scores. (Mc-Curdy, *Los Angeles Times*, January 31, 1969)

Because the book received wide attention and will likely stimulate more public discussion and policy decisions as well as much further research, it is imperative that its results be thoroughly evaluated and understood. Unfortunately, a complete understanding of the data and results are not obtainable from the published accounts alone.

Pygmalion in the Classroom can be severely criticized as a research report. We summarize our criticisms briefly here and then return to each in more detail. The RJ report is misleading. The text and tables are inconsistent, conclusions are overdramatized, and variables are given prejudicial labels. The three concluding chapters represent only superficial, and frequently inaccurate, attempts to deal with the study's flaws. Descriptions of design, basic data, and analysis are incomplete. The sampling plan is not spelled out in detail. Frequency distributions are lacking for either raw or IQ scores. Comparisons between text and appendix tables are hampered by the use of different subgroupings of the data and the absence of intermediate analysis-of-variance tables. Many tables and graphs show only differences between difference scores, i.e., gain for the experimental group minus gain for the control group. There are technical inaccuracies: charts and graphs are frequently drawn in a misleading way and the p-value or significance level is incorrectly defined and used. Statistical discussions are frequently oversimplified or completely incorrect (some of the statistical questions are considered in later sections).

In short, our criticisms can be stated in the more general words of D. Huff (1954):

The fault is in the filtering-down process from the researcher through the sensational or ill-informed writer to the reader who fails to miss the figures that have disappeared in the process.

Interpretations and Conclusions

Conclusions are frequently overstated and do not always agree from place to place in the book. Text and tables are not always in agreement. Again, our concern is well stated by Huff (1954, p. 131):

When assaying a statistic, watch out for a switch somewhere between the raw figure and the conclusion. One thing is all too often reported as another.

RJ use labels for their dependent variables that presume interpretations before effects are found, a practice especially to be condemned in publications aimed at the general public. "Intellectual growth" is used in referring to the simple difference between a child's pretest IQ score and his IQ score on a posttest. It is questionable whether simple gain from first to a later testing (with some adjustments for age) using the same test represents anything so global as intellectual growth.

The difference in gains shown by the experimental group over the control group is described as an "expectancy advantage." This term presupposes that the difference is always positive. In fact it is not. What particular "advantage" or "benefit" accrues to the child showing a large gain score is not made clear. Words like "special" and "magic" are also frequently used to refer to experimental children, when less provocative terms would serve as well.

Looking at RJ's main results for Total IQ, as reported in their Table 7-1 (see our Table 1), the first and second grade experimental groups show a large, significant expectancy advantage, the fourth graders show a small, nonsignificant advantage, the third and fifth graders show no difference and the sixth graders show a small, nonsignificant disadvantage. So RJ's table reports an "expectancy advantage" for the first and second graders (and possibly the fourth graders) and reports no "expectancy advantage" for the other grades. The significant "expectancy advantage" reported by RJ is thus based only on the 19 first and second graders in the experimental group. But RJ conclude:

We find increasing expectancy advantage as we go from the sixth to the first grade. . . . (p. 74)†

Here is how RJ describe the results elsewhere in the text:

When the entire school benefitted as in Total IQ and Reasoning IQ, all three tracks benefitted. (p. 78)†

When teachers expected that certain children would show greater intellectual development, these children did show greater intellectual development. (p. 82)†

The evidence presented in the last two chapters suggests rather strongly that children who are expected by their teachers to gain intellectually in fact do show greater intellectual gains after one year than do children of whom such gains are not expected. (p. 121)†

After the first year of the experiment a significant expectancy advantage was found, and it was especially great among children of the first and second grades. (p. 176)†

There is thus a clear tendency to overgeneralize the findings. When the authors are explaining away the results of *contradictory* experiments, however, the conclusions sound quite different:

The finding that only the younger children profited after one year from their teachers' favorable expectations helps us to understand better the [negative] results of two other experimenters. . . . (p. 84)†

The results of our own study suggest that after one year, fifth graders may not show the effects of teacher expectations though first and second graders do. (p. 84)†

Another important inconsistency is between the form of analysis and the stated conclusions. All analyses were done in terms of means, yet conclusions are stated in terms of individuals; for example ". . . when the entire school benefitted . . . ." or ". . . these children did show greater intellectual development." That is, the analyses performed by RJ could only show that average gains by experimental children were larger than average gains by control children, but RJ's statements imply that each individual experimental child gained and that these gains were all larger than those shown by any control group child.

There is a strong presumption throughout the book that teacher expectations have an effect. Contrary evidence is explained away. RJ cite other studies which in general did not support the conclusions drawn in this book. The discussion of these adverse findings de-emphasizes the possibility that teacher expectations have little effect on IQ scores and becomes almost absurd with references to all possible alternative hypotheses—"there is such an effect, but . . . . " (RJ, p. 57)†

One of RJ's closing chapters takes steps toward answering specific methodological criticisms. Unfortunately, much of this discussion is superficial and some is incorrect. (See later chapters on technical inaccuracies, design and sampling, and reliability.) RJ's chapter also offers speculation on possible processes of intentional and unintentional influence between the teachers and students, but fails to face the full implications of the fact that after the study the teachers could not remember the names on the original lists of "bloomers" and reported having scarcely glanced at the list.

RJ's last chapter provides a capsule summary and some general implications. It is here that the inadequacy of statistical summaries of these data should be clearly specified. But it is not. The reader expecting careful conclusions is given overdramatized generalities instead.

Tables, Figures, and Charts

Even with a faulty text, a reader should be able to examine the basic figures, tables, and analyses and draw his own conclusions. Clearly in a massive study, we cannot demand that an author include *all* the data, or a complete set of analysis-of-variance tables, etc. RJ indeed included many appendix tables of summary data. What then is wrong?

Nowhere can the reader see the distributions of pretest or posttest scores, the relationship between pretest and posttest scores, or the detailed results of any of the analyses. The tables in the body of the text show mean gain or "excess of gain" from pretest to posttest for treatment groups in breakdowns by grade, sex, track, or some combination of factors. Excess of gain is mean gain by the experimental group minus mean gain by the corresponding control group. This obscures the fact that some of the startling gains were made by children whose pretest IQs were far below reasonable levels for normal school children. Examination of alternative hypotheses, such as "that children higher (or lower) to begin with gain more," or "that unreliability may have contributed to spurious results," is hampered. Means and standard deviations for pretest, posttest, and gain are shown in the appendix but not for the same breakdowns as shown in the text. (In addition, standard deviations must be multiplied by $\sqrt{n/n-1}$ before use in a t-test since RJ apparently defined $s^2 = \sum(x_i - \bar{x})^2/n$ instead of using $s^2 = \sum(x_i - \bar{x})^2/(n-1)$.) Selected means or standard deviations to compare with text tables, such as Table 7-1 which shows a breakdown by grade, can be obtained with some computation. But for RJ tables such as Table 7-5 showing breakdown by sex, it is impossible to obtain mean pretest or posttest scores from data supplied in the book. Since no analysis-of-variance tables are shown, the reader must rely on statements like "The interaction term was not very significant ($p <$ .15) . . . ." (RJ, p. 77)† However, there were several analyses of variance, with different combinations of factors yielding different results, so p-values quoted in the text were all obtained from different analysis-of-variance calculations. The reader is left uncertain as to which results were obtained in what analysis and cannot reconstruct tables of means to interpret each effect for himself.

Since final interpretations of the results and the validity of many of the statistical procedures RJ employed rests on the score distributions and the relationships of pre to post scores, the reader would hope to find tables, histograms, and scatterplots to enable him to examine the data more closely, at least for the main subsets of data. At the very least, the authors should be able to assure the reader that they have examined the data in this light and are satisfied. But no histograms or frequency distributions of individual scores are provided or mentioned. If these were displayed, the reader would notice that Total IQ scores range from 39 to 202, Reasoning IQ scores range from 0 to 262, and Verbal IQ scores range from 46 to 300. (See Chapter IV for a discussion of the meaning of extreme scores like these.) There are also no scatterplots showing relationships between pretest and posttest scores.

Of the nine figures in RJ Chapters 7-9, eight are drawn in a misleading way; Huff calls graphs like these "gee-whiz" graphs. RJ Figure 7-2, which also appeared in *Scientific American* (RJ, 1968a), is mislabeled, does not state that its impressive percentages are based on a total of only 19 children in the experimental

FIGURE 2a: PERCENTAGES OF FIRST AND SECOND GRADERS
GAINING TEN, TWENTY, or THIRTY TOTAL IQ
POINTS
(Reprinted from RJ, their figure 7-2, p. 76)†

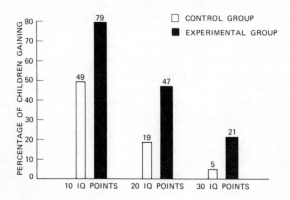

FIGURE 2b: RJ FIGURE 7-2 REDRAWN TO ELIMINATE REPETITION
(Note that "gains" actually varied from -17 to +65)

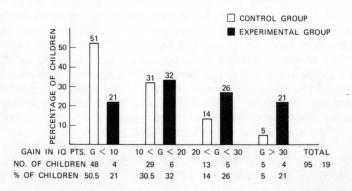

GAIN IN IQ PTS.	G < 10		10 < G < 20		20 < G < 30		G > 30		TOTAL	
NO. OF CHILDREN	48	4	29	6	13	5	5	4	95	19
% OF CHILDREN	50.5	21	30.5	32	14	26	5	21		

group, with the 4 children gaining 30 or more points included with those gaining 20 or more points who in turn have been included with the children gaining 10 or more points. Our Figure 2b shows the information in RJ's Figure 7-2 redrawn to eliminate overlapping or repetition of information and inaccurate labeling.

RJ Figures 8-1, 8-2, 9-1, and 9-2 all are drawn with false zero lines, overemphasizing apparent gains and differences in gain. For example, in RJ Figure 8-1 the line of zero gain is in the middle of the chart and the entire scale displayed on the graph runs from -0.5 to $+0.8$ grade points based on a scale from 0 for "F" to 4 for "A." The choice of scale makes the gains and differences in gains look large when, in fact, most are considerably less than one grade point. Our Figures 3a and 3b show RJ's Figure 8-1 and the same figure redrawn appropriately. Figures such as 8-1, 8-2, 9-1, and 9-2 should be drawn with the zero line strongly indicated and all gains originating from it.

The four "process of blooming" charts (RJ Figures 9-3 through 9-6) not only display floating zero lines and elastic scales from one IQ measure to another, but particular measures are drawn on different scales in each chart so that comparisons between charts are not possible. (Scales for the IQ differences are 0 to 5, -3 to 12, 0 to 12.5, and 0 to 6 respectively.) More important, the "expectancy advantage" computed at each time point is based on a different set of children, since there are missing data and subject losses along the way. Finally, all the charts indicate no "expectancy advantage" at Time 1 (the pretest). Since the experiment had not begun there are no gains to compare, but in fact the two groups did *not* have the same average pretest scores. For example, for the Total IQ chart in Figure 1 the experimental group had average pretest scores 4.9 IQ points higher than the control group in the lower grades and 2.4 IQ points higher in the upper grades (these numbers obtained from our Table 20 in Appendix A).

Technical Inaccuracies

Books intended for use by students should be free from technical inaccuracies. One striking deficiency here is RJ's misuse of *p*-value. The concept of *p*-value or significance level is incorrectly defined and interpreted through the book. In the preface, *p*-value is defined incorrectly:

". . . there often will be a letter *p* with some decimal value, usually .05 or .01 or .001. These decimals give the probability that the finding reported could have occurred by chance. For example, in comparing

FIGURE 3a: GAINS IN READING GRADES IN SIX GRADES
(Reprinted from RJ, their figure 8-1, p. 100)†

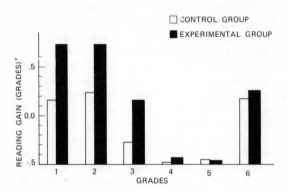

FIGURE 3b: RJ FIGURE 8-1 REDRAWN WITH GAINS BEGINNING
AT ZERO

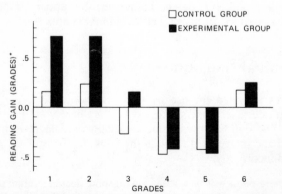

*These are coded teacher's marks (A = 4, B = 3, C = 2,
D = 1, F or U = 0), not grade equivalent scores

two groups the statistical significance of the difference in scores may be reported as $t = 2.50$, $p < .01$, one-tailed. This means that the likelihood was less than 1 in 100 that the difference found could have occurred by chance." (p. ix)†

This definition should read: this means that the likelihood was less than 1 in 100 that the difference found *or one larger* could have occurred by chance *if the difference between the population means were zero and all the assumptions necessary for the test to be valid were satisfied.* The trouble with RJ's definition is its implication that the observed difference *is* the true difference, that because this particular difference is unlikely to have occurred by chance it must be real. The *p*-value does not tell us how close an observed difference is likely to be to the true difference. It simply identifies the likelihood of a more extreme result than the one observed, given that the null hypothesis is true. For example, if a *t*-test based on a difference in sample means of, say, 10.2 yields $p < .01$, one-tail, this means that the probability of observing a difference in sample means as large or larger than 10.2 is less than .01 if in fact there is no real difference in population means and all the assumptions necessary for the test to be valid are satisfied. The "true difference" need not be anywhere near 10.2. For example, the probability of observing a difference in sample means by chance more extreme than 10.2 if the "true difference" were 6.8 is about .22.

RJ seem also to use *p*-value as a measure of strength of effect, an indication of the size and practical importance of mean differences. They do not use a standard *p*-value such as .05, preferring to quote values ranging from .25 to .00002 thus encouraging the reader to conclude that *p*-values of .001 indicate truer, larger, more important effects than *p*-values of .01. The *p*-value is not a useful measure of the size or importance of an observed treatment effect for individuals because it depends on the sample sizes involved as well as the actual size of the difference. Small differences of no practical importance can be shown statistically significant at a small *p*-value if the sample size is large enough. Conversely, large observed differences may not be statistically significant if the sample size is small. Procedures which can be used to assess the size of treatment effects include: confidence interval for the differences in means, histograms showing the relative positions of control group scores and experimental group scores, percent of individuals misclassified, measures of statistical association such as $_\omega^2$ (Hays, 1963), and linear regression analysis showing the percent of variance accounted for by treatment relative to other factors.

Most importantly, however, it is usually meaningless to quote particular *p*-values less than .01 since the actual distribution of a statistic such as t in a real problem will seldom be well approximated by the tabled distribution far enough into the tails (see our later section on reliability) for small p-values to be meaningful.

RJ devote nine pages to a discussion of the higher gains in reading grades shown by the experimental or "special" children. Yet they state:

> When the entire school was considered, there was only one of the eleven school subjects in which there was a significant difference between the grade-point gains shown by the special children and the control-group children. (p. 99)†

Why is so much emphasis placed on results for one out of eleven school subjects? A series of eleven independent t-tests at the 10% level referred to by RJ can be expected to produce at least one significant difference by chance even though there is no true difference in any of the eleven. In fact, the probability of obtaining at least one significant difference by chance under these circumstances is .6862*. Of course, these sets of grades are not independent and the probability of obtaining at least one significant result by chance will be smaller than .6862 but will undoubtedly be considerably larger than .10.

In a footnote, RJ argue that:

> Even allowing for the fact that reading was the only school subject to reach a $p < .10$ of a total of eleven school subjects, these obtained p's for reading seem too low to justify our ascribing them to chance. If the eleven subjects were independent, which they were not . . . we might expect on the average to find by chance one $p < .09$, and that expected p is about ten times larger than those obtained when classrooms served as sampling units. (p. 118-119)†

The problem of "expected p-values" needs further examination. First, no matter how small the p-value is, the difference may not be real; there is always the chance that a rare event has occurred. Second, what is the probability of a very small p-value given that the p-value is less than .10? It is easiest to examine this question for the sign test on seventeen classes, for which the obtained p-value for reading scores was .0062. Given that $p < .10$, and that the probability of $E > C$ is one half, the probability that the p-value is less than or equal to .0062 is .0879. In other words, there is about a 9% chance of a p-value as small or smaller than .0062 given that $p < .10$. In such circumstances, a confidence interval for the difference in reading scores would provide more information about the practical importance of obtained results than any discussion of p-value.

---

*$P(t$ significant $|H_0) = .10$, P(no t significant $|H_0$, 11 independent t's)$= (.90)^{11}$, P(one or more t significant $|H_0) = 1-(.90)^{11} = .6862$.

III

Design and Sampling Problems

There are several problems inherent in the design of the RJ study and the sample finally obtained. We list them briefly and then discuss each in turn. The sampling plan, the procedure for assignment of children to treatment groups, is ill-defined. Little balance was designed into the study. A 20% subject loss from pretest to posttest reduces the generalizability of the study and raises the possibility of differential subject loss in experimental and control groups. Because of the uncertain sampling plan, the lack of balance and the possibility of nonrandom subject loss during the experiment, the fact that the experimental group showed higher pretest scores on the average, especially in the lower grades, suggests serious difficulties that attempts at statistical correction may not erase.

The details of a sampling plan provide the basis for subsequent statistical inference as well as for planning replications of a study. In addition, the sampling plan determines the population to which the results can be generalized, the unit of observation (individual or classroom), the comparability of experimental and control groups, and the factors which may be used in an analysis of variance. It is not clear from the RJ book just what the procedure for assignment to treatment groups was. According to the authors, a 20% random sample of the school's children was listed as "bloomers" to form the experimental group. However, ". . . it was felt to be more plausible if each teacher did not have exactly the same number or percentage of her class listed."(p. 70)† Thus, the number of experimental children in a classroom varied from one to nine. "For the same reason the proportion of either boys or girls on each teacher's list was allowed to vary from a minimum of 40% of the designated children to a maximum of 60% of the designated children."(p. 71)† Was this plan simple random

TABLE 2

Number of Children Taking the Basic Posttest

by Classroom and Treatment Group

Grade	Group	Track		
		Fast	Medium	Slow
1	C	17	15	16
	E	1 (6%)	4 (21%)	2 (11%)
2	C	19	14	14
	E	6 (24%)	3 (18%)	3 (18%)
3	C	12	15	13
	E	8 (40%)	1 (6%)	5 (28%)
4	C	18	16	15
	E	5 (22%)	3 (16%)	4 (21%)
5	C	16	-	10
	E	5 (24%)	-	4 (29%)
6	C	20	13	12
	E	4 (17%)	4 (24%)	3 (20%)
All Grades	C	102	73	80
	E	29 (22%)	15 (17%)	21 (21%)

sampling, or random sampling stratified by sex and classroom, or some compromise solution? It makes a difference in our choice of analysis. Perhaps simple randomization was followed by a nonrandom reassignment procedure to fit specifications; the authors do not say. In the final analysis can we actually assume random assignment to treatments?

The major difficulty with the RJ design is the imbalance deliberately created to make the experimental condition plausible for the teachers. With highly variable human subjects and a small experimental group, it is especially important that the experimental and control groups be comparable on as many factors as possible. Statistical inference at the end of the experiment will rest on the finding that the experimental and control groups differ by more than could be expected on the basis of inherent variability. If groups differ for reasons other than the experimental treatment variable, results may be confounded and interpretation rendered impossible. A main objective of experimental design is to control sources of variability so that no confounding impedes interpretation.

As a result of subject loss during the experiment as well as original inequalities, the number of children in each classroom and treatment group available for the basic posttest varies as shown in Table 2. The percent of children in the experimental group from each classroom is also shown. The lack of equality in the number of experimental children per classroom means that some classes have too few experimental children to make analysis within classrooms feasible. The addition of sex as a factor in the analysis immediately creates empty cells. RJ's approach of combining across other factors to do analyses of variance on such cross-classifications as treatment by sex, and treatment by sex by grade, necessitates combining over tracks and introduces confounding. In the first grade, for example, the experimental group comes mainly from the middle track while in the third grade the middle track is hardly represented at all; tracks are much more evenly represented in the control group. (When tracks are combined, the analyses of variance may yield misleading results; see the discussion accompanying Table 15 in Appendix A.)

In designing experiments like the one under discussion here, an appropriate procedure is first to match or block subjects on potentially important variables, like grade, sex, and classroom, and then to rely on random assignment of subjects to treatments *within blocks* to provide balance for other variables. This procedure insures that the groups are comparable on the blocked variables and thus equally representative of the population of interest. It is also advisable to check the adequacy of obtained balance in the subjects remaining in the experiment at the end; different experimental treatments can create differential dropout or loss rates

TABLE 3

Number of Children Taking Pretest and at Least One Posttest

	Pretest only	Pretest and at least one posttest	Total pretested
Control	79	305	384
Experimental	17	77	94
Total	96	382	478

among subjects, and this effect may dictate changes in the statistical analysis, as well as being of interest in its own right. Variables which have not been used in blocking may be included as factors in an analysis of variance only with considerable caution (see section on analysis of variance in unbalanced designs in Appendix A).

The plausibility of the lists of children expected to "bloom" is a crucial issue in an experiment of this type, but randomization and balance are also important. RJ could have taken some steps to achieve balance without giving every teacher a list including exactly the same number of names. The most important factor for balancing is perhaps ability track. Track assignments were made on the basis of reading ability by the previous year's teacher, after the administration of the TOGA pretest but without knowledge of these pretest IQs. There were three classes, representing the three tracks, at each grade level. Since classes apparently differed in size, assigning exactly the same proportion of children in each class would not have resulted in the same number of children on each list. If class size represented on the pretest is indicative of the whole experiment, total class size varied from 16 to 27; 20% of these classes would vary from three to five or six. It is questionable whether a teacher would notice that three in a class of 17 represents the same proportion as six in a class of 28. However, another possibility would have been to take a lower percentage of children from the fast track and a higher percentage of children from the slow track, since fast track children might be said to have already "bloomed." If all classes were of size 20, we might choose 15%, 20%, 25%, or three, four, and five experimental children in the fast, medium, and slow tracks, respectively.

With such a small experimental group it is difficult to achieve balance on sex also, but perhaps teachers could be told that the prediction is done separately for the two sexes so the lists contain equal numbers of boys and girls. There seems little reason for allowing the number of experimental children in a class to vary haphazardly from one to nine. When many children are lost to the experiment through attrition, the original balance may be partially lost, but this is no reason to ignore the question of balance at the beginning.

There is the possibility of a selection bias of unknown proportions. Although 478 children were given the pretest, only 382 or 80% were present for at least one posttest and were thus "included in the experiment" (see Table 3). RJ remark that "The ins and outs seldom belong to the high or top-achieving third of the school."(p. 63)† Thus the children remaining in the experiment cannot be considered a random sample of Oak School children and the results may not be representative of the reactions of the whole school population. In view of the high subject loss, it is doubtful that the experimental and control children can still be regarded as representing comparable groups. Although roughly the same proportion of experimental and control children were lost to the experiment, pretest scores on lost subjects were not available and it is impossible to tell whether both groups lost comparable children.

Given the uncertain sampling plan and large subject loss, it is disconcerting to note that, for those children remaining in the experiment, the pretest scores are consistently superior in the experimental group.

In spite of random allocation to the experimental condition, the children of the experimental group scored slightly higher in pretest IQ than did the children of the control group. This fact suggested the possibility that those children who were brighter to begin with might have shown the greater gains in intellectual performance.(p. 150)†

In Chapter 10, RJ explore this possibility using two different procedures: one involves correlations between pretest scores and gain scores; the second is based on post hoc matching of experimental and control children. They conclude:

These analyses suggest that the over-all significant effects of teachers' favorable expectations cannot be attributed to differences between the experimental- and control-group children in pretest IQ. (p. 151)†

But neither RJ procedure provides an adequate investigation of the possibility that children higher to begin with gained more. The correlation analysis is, in fact, incorrect. RJ state:

As one check on this hypothesis, the correlations were computed between children's initial pretest IQ scores and the magnitude of their gains in IQ after one year. If those who were brighter to begin with showed greater gains in IQ, the correlations would be positive. In general, the over-all correlations were negative; for total IQ r = − .23 (*p* < .001); for verbal IQ r = − .04 (not significant); and for reasoning IQ, r = − .48 (*p* < .001). (p. 150)†

Actually, the correlation between pretest scores and gain scores can generally be expected to be negative. If X_i represents the pretest scores, and Y_i the posttest scores; their variances are σ_X^2 and σ_Y^2, and their correlation is ρ. Then the correlation between gain scores, $Y_i - X_i$ and pretest scores X_i is

$$\rho_{Y-X,X} = \frac{\rho\sigma_Y - \sigma_X}{\sqrt{(\sigma_Y - \sigma_X)^2 + 2(1-\rho)\sigma_X\sigma_Y}} .$$

Thus, $\rho_{Y-X,X}$ can be positive only if $\rho > \sigma_X/\sigma_Y$. Since σ_X/σ_Y should seldom be much smaller than 1.0, we see that the correlation between gain scores and pretest scores will generally be negative. (If, for example $\sigma_X = \sigma_Y$ and $\rho = .68$ which is a situation representative of the RJ data—see Tables 4, 5, 6—then $\rho_{Y-X,X} = -.4$).

Clearly, correlations between pretest scores and gain scores are determined by the correlation between pretest scores and posttest scores and cannot be used to investigate whether those who were brighter to begin with gained more. If pretest and posttest scores have a linear relationship and those with higher pretest scores gain more, the slope of the regression equation of posttest on pretest will be greater than unity. If those with higher pretest scores gained a great deal more, one might expect to find a nonlinear relationship between pre- and posttest. Referring to our reanalysis section in Appendix A, note that the slope is generally less than unity; it is larger than unity for grades 5 and 6 Total and Verbal IQ and grades 3 and 4 Verbal IQ (Tables 9 and 10). Note however, that Figures 11 through 19 show nonlinear effects produced by a few children with high pretest scores and large gains.

RJ's second procedure was to match experimental and control group children within classrooms on pretest scores and to compute an "expectancy advantage" for each matched pair. Post hoc matching can be useful only when close, objectively chosen matches are possible. Since the experimental group was only one-fourth the size of the control group, choosing a control child to match each experimental child must involve subjective decisions. Also, the fact that 13 of the 65 experimental children were left unmatched indicates a lack of comparability of the two groups. Our reanalysis section in Appendix A presents some further evidence on the difficulties involved in post hoc matching.

IV

Measurement Problems

For the main purposes of their study, RJ chose TOGA, a group intelligence test which purportedly does not require reading ability. RJ obtained individual IQ scores for each testing and defined changes in these scores over time as "intellectual growth." TOGA forms K-2, 2-4, and 4-6 were used. On the pretest K-2 was administered to the kindergarten and first grade classes, form 2-4 was administered to the second and third grades, and form 4-6 was administered to the fourth and fifth grades. On the second and third tests during the following year all children were retested with the same test form (grade designation used by RJ was that at basic posttest). On the fourth test, two years after the pretest, those who had been in kindergarten, second grade, or fourth grade on the pretest were again tested with the same TOGA form while the other children were tested with the next higher-level form. These IQ tests were multiple choice with five choices for each item; forms K-2 and 2-4 each had 63 items, 35 verbal and 28 reasoning, form 4-6 had 85 items. Thus for example, children in kindergarten on the pretest, first grade for second and third tests, and second grade for the fourth test received form K-2 all four times, while children in the first grade on the pretest, second grade for the basic posttest, and third grade for the last test received form K-2 the first three times and form 2-4 for the fourth time.

Among the most important questions to be asked, here as in any research project, are: What is being measured? How is it being measured? How accurately is it being measured? What scale of measurement is being used? In this section we examine the IQ scores actually obtained by children in Oak school, and questions of norming, reliability, and validity for these measurements.

Scores and Norms

Problems began with the decision to rely *solely* on TOGA. Examination of the manual suggests that the test has not been fully normed for the youngest children, especially for children from lower socioeconomic backgrounds. In addition, it was administered to separate classes by the teachers themselves, a fact which raises doubts about standardization of procedure. A review of the test manual shows that for grades K-2 the procedure is regarded more as a class project than as a test. Although the teacher reads each item in the verbal subtest, in the reasoning portion children are left on their own with only minimal instruction or guidance from the teacher. There appears to have been no attempt to train the teachers in test administration, to check the adequacy of administration, or to determine whether the test and its instructions and procedure were understood by the subjects. With kindergartners and first graders, in particular, it is doubtful that any closely timed group test can be regarded as an adequate measure of intellectual status.

All computations were based on IQ scores—a transformation of the raw scores based on norm groups and the age of the child. The total raw score distribution on form K-2 for example has a possible range of 0 to 63 points. Examining the conversion table, one notes that a difference in raw scores of one item on TOGA will result in an IQ difference (for children of the same age) of about 2 points near the center of the distribution, up to 8 points at the bottom of the scale, and 60 points at the top.

According to the manual, TOGA IQ scores were normed so that for school children the mean IQ should be 100 (although it might be lower for some socioeconomic groups) and the standard deviation should be 16 or 17. Thus 95% of the children should be in the range 67 to 133. A detailed table of mental ages corresponding to each raw score from one to the maximum possible is provided in the manual. In a technical report accompanying TOGA, norms showing mental age extrapolated up to 26.6 and down to zero are provided. As R.L. Thorndike (1969) notes elsewhere, however, extrapolations outside the norm sample range are of questionable value. Indeed, the tables showing IQ scores for each raw score and age are not extrapolated beyond IQs of 60 and 160. Thus although it is possible to obtain IQs of 0 to 200 or more using information provided in the manual, the manual implicitly discourages use of IQs lower than 60 or higher than 160, which should occur very rarely in any case.

One simple check on the adequacy of the IQ scores provided by TOGA would be a comparison of the score distribution obtained

TABLE 4

Pretest Scores

All Pretested Children with at Least One Posttest

Total IQ

Grade	N	Mean	Standard Deviation	Minimum	Maximum
1	63	90.0	19.4	39	130
2	63	94.7	15.8	59	133
1 & 2	126	92.3	17.9	39	133
3 & 4	131	104.3	17.4	64	158
5 & 6	125	99.2	18.4	56	152

Reasoning IQ

Grade	N	Mean	Standard Deviation	Minimum	Maximum
1	63	58.0	36.8	0	111
2	63	89.1	21.6	39	133
1 & 2	126	73.5	34.1	0	133
3 & 4	131	99.5	19.5	56	167
5 & 6	125	96.6	20.3	52	158

Verbal IQ

Grade	N	Mean	Standard Deviation	Minimum	Maximum
1	63	105.7	21.2	54	183
2	63	99.4	16.1	50	133
1 & 2	126	102.6	19.2	50	183
3 & 4	131	109.7	22.2	68	171
5 & 6	125	102.6	24.4	46	165

for the "Oak School" children with those of the norming groups. RJ provide no score distributions in either text or appendix, although examining RJ Tables A-1, A-2, and A-3 in the appendix we find pretest Total IQ means within treatment group of 60.5, 76.9, 79.9 for some low track classrooms. The pretest mean for Reasoning IQ was 58.0 for the entire first grade; in the first grade control group, Reasoning pretest means were 30.8 and 47.2 for slow and medium track, respectively. It should be noted that, at one time, children with IQs below 70 were officially described as feeble-minded. Those below 40 were labeled "imbeciles." Today,

TABLE 5

Basic Posttest Scores

			Total IQ		
Grade	N	Mean	Standard Deviation	Minimum	Maximum
1 & 2	114	103.4	18.4	67	202
3 & 4	115	107.7	20.1	57	165
5 & 6	91	112.3	22.8	63	171
			Reasoning IQ		
1 & 2	114	102.3	29.2	39	211
3 & 4	115	103.6	28.5	0	262
5 & 6	91	116.5	29.7	67	251
			Verbal IQ		
1 & 2	114	108.6	21.1	71	221
3 & 4	115	116.1	31.9	69	300
5 & 6	108	113.2	31.0	59	249

a score of 75 or below usually identifies individuals for special EMR (educable mentally retarded) classes. Since IQ scores as high as 60 could easily be obtained by "guessing" on form K-2 (see below) IQ scores as low as these must include random or systematically incorrect responses and unattempted items (an IQ of 63 for a six-year-old represents 12 correct out of 63 multiple choice items). Some IQ means seemed inconsistent with the tracking classification; for the third grade control group, fast, medium, and slow track pretest total IQ means were 98.4, 102.2, 100.3 respectively. Pretest means for different forms of TOGA also seemed inconsistent; first and second graders had a mean total IQ of 92.3, third and fourth graders of 104.3 and fifth and sixth graders of 99.2.

As a consequence, our first step was to examine the score distributions in detail. Histograms of Total IQ, Verbal IQ, and Reasoning IQ scores on pretest and basic posttest for each grade are shown in Figures 4-9. Means, standard deviations, and maximum and minimum scores are shown in Tables 4 and 5.

Notice the pretest Reasoning IQs of zero in the first grade (Figure 6), the posttest Total IQs of 202 in the second grade, the posttest Verbal IQs of 221, 249, 300, and the posttest Reasoning IQs of 251, 262.

Since Total IQ scores on the pretest were so low for first and second graders, it is interesting to compare the obtained distribution with that to be expected if children merely "guessed." TOGA form K-2 is a multiple choice test with five choices for each of 63 items. If we define "guessing" to mean that a child selects at random one of the five choices and each choice is made with probability 1/5, then raw scores on the test should have a binomial distribution with $n = 63$, $p = 1/5$. The pretest raw score distribution for first and second graders is shown in Figure 10. The histogram shown with dotted lines gives expected raw scores drawn as if, for example, one-sixth (or 19) of the children merely picked their answers at random. The average number of items that were correct by guessing would be 13. Notice how many of the children did have pretest scores in the "guessing" range. Note that a raw score of 8 in a child of age six yields an IQ of 50, a raw score of 13 an IQ of 67, a raw score of 20 an IQ of 83.

Actually, it is rare that all children attempt all items. In this experiment, where teacher influences on subsequent test performance are of central importance, detailed data on test items answered incorrectly vs. items left unanswered at each testing should have been provided. It would be helpful in hypothesizing further about the nature of teacher effects, if found. Thorndike (1969) notes that the main influence of extra encouragement by the teacher might well be to increase the number of items attempted, even by guessing. RJ provide no data on this question, but Rosenthal notes elsewhere (1969, p. 690) that ". . . low IQs were earned because very few items were attempted by many of the children."

Reliability Questions

Examination of the score distributions reveals many extreme IQ scores less than 60 or greater than 160; RJ do not discuss these strange scores and have included them in standard analyses without comment. How stable are the IQ scores obtained across time? Test-retest correlations seem low at times especially for Reasoning IQ (see our Table 6, RJ's Table A-30). Looking at individual score sequences (using the data sent us by RJ) we noticed many instances of instability of IQ scores across time. A few examples of the more striking cases include one child with successive Total IQs of 55, 102, 95, 104; another with 84, 120, 107, 105; another with 88, 85, 128, 101; and another with 97, 88, 100, 127. For Verbal IQ we find sequences 54, 121, 101, 74; and 125, 87, 86, 68; and 167, 293, 174, 130. For Reasoning IQ, the sequences 0, 77, 82, 143; and 17, 148, 110, 112; and 111, 89, 208, 125; and 114, 81, 88, 106 appear. In view of the fact that children were

FIGURE 4: PRETEST TOTAL IQ DISTRIBUTION BY GRADE

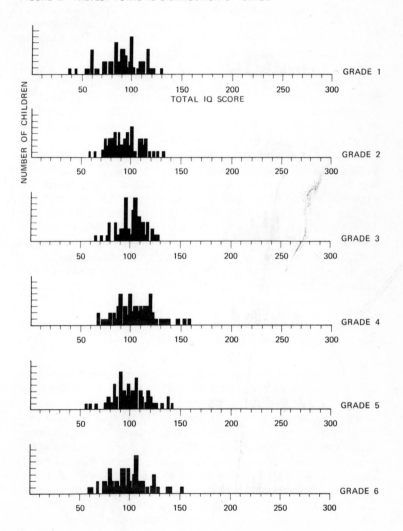

FIGURE 5: PRETEST VERBAL IQ DISTRIBUTION BY GRADE

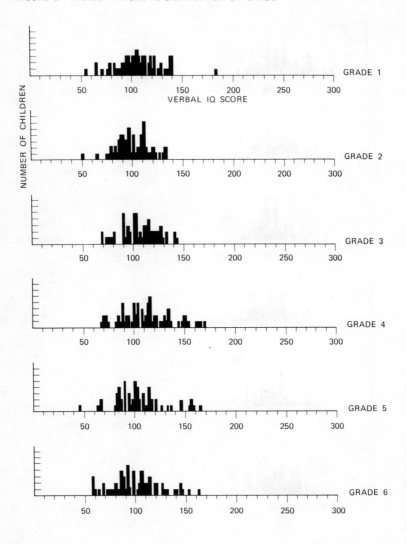

FIGURE 6: PRETEST REASONING IQ DISTRIBUTION BY GRADE

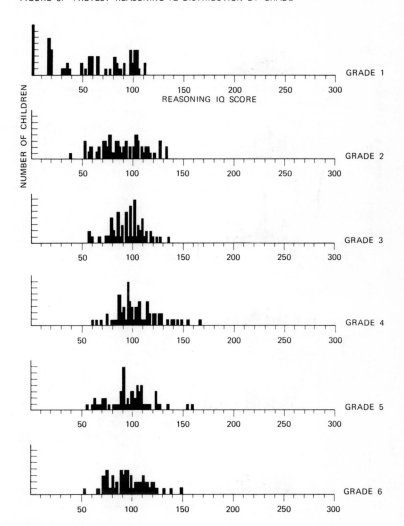

FIGURE 7: POSTTEST TOTAL IQ DISTRIBUTION BY GRADE

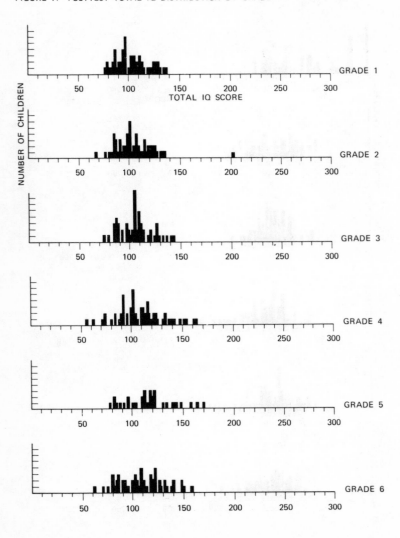

FIGURE 8: POSTTEST VERBAL IQ DISTRIBUTION BY GRADE

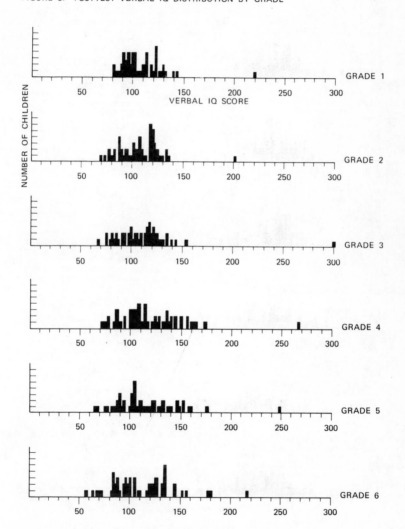

FIGURE 9: POSTTEST REASONING IQ DISTRIBUTION BY GRADE

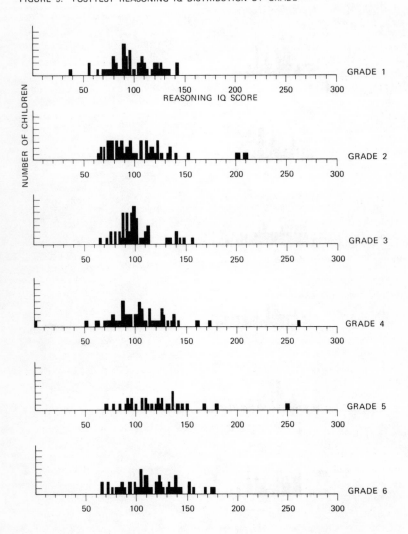

tested three and four times with exactly the same test we should expect greater stability than this. A partial explanation of the unreliability of these scores is contained in the TOGA manual: "For second grade children of average or above-average ability, TOGA 2-4 will usually provide more reliable test scores."

The sections of the RJ book devoted to discussion of the reliability problem are unsatisfactory. RJ state:

In fact, on a more rigorous basis, it can be shown that the less reliable a test, the more difficult it is to obtain systematic, significant differences between groups when such differences do, in fact, exist. In summary, there seems to be no way in which the "unreliability" of our group measure of intelligence could account for our results although it could, in principle, account for the results not having been still more dramatic. (p. 149)†

The problems of test unreliability . . . were discussed and found wanting as explanations of our results. (p. 179)†

These statements are exaggerated and oversimplified. First, all statements about the effects of unreliability on a statistical test must be based on a probability model which describes the unreliability. The standard model for the reliability of gain scores is that pretest scores X and posttest scores Y come from a bivariate normal distribution with correlation coefficient ρ. (That is, X and Y both have normal distributions and are linearly related.) Thus "unreliability" is the same for all IQ levels, and the reliability, ρ, as well as the variances of X and Y, is the same for both experimental and control groups.

Under this standard model, it is true as RJ note, that the greater the unreliability of the test the larger the variance of gain scores and the larger the sample size necessary to show significance for true differences of a certain size between means of the groups. Therefore, unreliability in a test increases the probability of Type II errors, that is, it increases the probability of finding no significant difference when true differences exist. However, it does not reduce the probability of a Type I error; that is fixed by the experimenter. The probability of obtaining a statistically significant difference between experimental and control groups when no real difference exists is still equal to the *p*-value and is unaffected by the size of ρ. Furthermore, this is by no means the only possible model for unreliability and may not accurately describe the RJ data. The standard model maintains that IQ scores or gain scores for both control and experimental groups are drawn from the same distribution except that the means may be different. If the scores

FIGURE 10: FIRST AND SECOND GRADE PRETEST SCORES

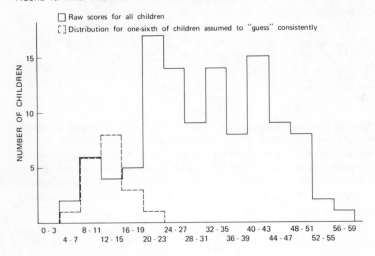

in the two groups come from distributions with different variances, different skewness, different kurtosis, then the actual probability of obtaining a significant difference in sample means when no difference in population means exists may be quite different from the nominal significance level of the test.

When two groups have markedly different sample sizes and markedly different variances, the actual significance level of a t-test may be quite different from the nominal significance level (see R. M. Elashoff, 1968). For example, if both the experimental and control groups have normal distributions with a ratio of sample sizes (n_c/n_e) of 5 and a ratio of variances (σ_c^2/σ_e^2) of .5, then in large samples and for a nominal significance level of .05, the actual significance level of the t-test would be .12. That is, to perform a t-test at the 5% level of significance, we reject the null hypothesis if the observed t-value is greater than 1.96. When $n_c/n_e = 5$ and $\sigma_c^2/\sigma_e^2 = .5$ the actual probability of observing a t value greater than 1.96 under the null hypothesis is 12%. In the RJ experiment for the combined first and second grades, n_c/n_e is about 5 and the observed ratio of variances for Total IQ gain scores is $s_c^2/s_e^2 = .62$, consequently p-values quoted by RJ for comparisons in the lower grades are probably spuriously low.

Validity Questions

RJ do not provide a satisfactory discussion of the validity of their measure of "intellectual growth." "Intellectual growth" must mean more than changing a few answers the second time through a single test. Other mental ability information available from the school or obtainable without undue additional effort could have been used to examine the validity of the TOGA scores. A usual procedure in questions of construct validity is to show correlations between the measure in question and other indices presumed to represent the same or similar construct. RJ did not attempt to relate the TOGA scores to other acknowledged intelligence measures. The supporting evidence they introduce consists of changes in teacher grades, assessments of behavior made at one point in time, and a substudy of Iowa Tests of Basic Skills for the fifth and sixth grades. RJ report significant differences between experimental and control groups on one school subject out of eleven and three of nine "classroom behavior" indices. None of these differences, however, were as large as one point on scales of 1 to 4 for grades and 1 to 9 for behavior. No correlations between IQ and grades or behavior or achievement are shown; no correlations between gains in IQ and gains in grade points, changes in behavior, or gains in achievement are shown. In short, it is not clear how valid the TOGA IQ measures themselves are as a measure of intelligence or achievement or how valid changes in TOGA IQ scores are as a measure of intellectual growth.

In view of the conditions of test administration, pretest scores in the lower grades very likely involve variance due to differences in listening to instructions, perseverance, or resistance to distraction. These influences are particularly likely in the reasoning subtest, which is not teacher paced as the verbal subtest items are. Interpretations based on these influences would at least make the low pretest scores more credible, but a rather different interpretation of expectancy effects would also be required.

Rosenthal (1969) elsewhere argues that TOGA's validity is demonstrated by its correlation (.65) with ability track placement the following year. A test could predict a gross, three-level judgment of academic status well and still be nearly useless as a measure of individual intellectual ability or growth. Thus, such a correlation in no way validates the scale of measurement or its meaning and that is the question at issue here.

TABLE 6

Test-retest Correlations

Pretest to Basic Posttest

	Control	Experimental
1st & 2nd Grades		
Total IQ	.66	.72
Verbal IQ	.73	.70
Reasoning IQ	.45	.50
3rd & 4th Grades		
Total IQ	.77	.87
Verbal IQ	.71	.74
Reasoning IQ	.57	.74
5th & 6th Grades		
Total IQ	.84	.87
Verbal IQ	.83	.85
Reasoning IQ	.63	.48

Another check on the relationship of the TOGA scores to other assessments of the children might be provided by considering track transfers. RJ do not discuss transfers of children between ability tracks, so the reader is permitted the dubious assumption that no students changed track across the study's two-year span even though some IQs changed more than 100 points. In fact, some track transfers did occur. According to information received from RJ the track location used in the analyses was track location as of January 1965, or about the time of the first posttest. There were indeed track changes during the experiment, however, as shown in Table 7. The relative numbers of control and experimental group children who changed tracks is consistent with their proportions in the experiment. Since the experimental group does not show a significantly greater proportion of upward changes than the control group, track changes do not support the contention that experimental children "benefited more" than control children.

TABLE 7

Number of Children Changing Tracks

During 1964-1965

	Control	Experimental	
No change	285	73	358
Up	14	4	18
Down	6	0	6
Total	305	77	382

There is another difficulty created by the information that the track location is *not* that corresponding to the initial assignment of children within each class; we no longer know which class to compare these children with. Children have changed from cell to cell of the design during the experiment.

Another validity question concerns the experiment in general. In any experiment, one must be assured that the treatment conditions actually represent the intended variables. Particularly where incidental processes are of interest or where deception is involved, some procedure should be included to "cross-validate" the experimental effect. RJ took at least a first step in this direction by including a teacher interview and memory test at the end of the experiment. However, RJ fail to face the full implications of their results:

While all teachers recalled glancing at their lists, most felt they paid little or no attention to them. Many teachers threw their lists away after glancing at them. (p. 154)†

Also, teachers could not recall with any degree of success which children had been expected to bloom and which had not.

A memory test administered to the teachers showed that they could not recall accurately, nor even choose accurately from a larger list of names, the names of their own pupils designated as experimental-group children. (p. 69)†

Evidently the Pygmalion effect, if any, is an extremely subtle and elusive phenomenon that acts through teachers without conscious awareness on their part.

V

Overview of
Analysis and Conclusions

The basic aim of analysis in the RJ experiment was to assess the relationship between pretest and posttest scores in the experimental and control groups, to locate any statistically significant differences between the groups, and to assess the practical importance of any significant differences observed. RJ based their analyses on the five-way classification of treatment x grade x track x sex x minority group status. They performed unweighted means analyses of variance using several different subsets of the classification factors because of unequal cell sizes and the prevalence of small or empty cells. The criterion was simple gain in IQ from pretest to posttest. Pretest to basic posttest (T_3—T_1) was of primary interest but pretest to first posttest (T_2—T_1) and pretest to follow-up posttest (T_4—T_1) were also included.

We considered the RJ analysis inadequate in the choice of analytic procedure, in the choice of criterion measure, and in the attention paid to the basic data. Data analysis is an endeavor that must justify all that has preceded it in the experiment; analytic procedures must be chosen with the details of particular substantive hypotheses and the intricacies of appropriate statistical machinery clearly in mind. When considerable time and effort have been invested in the design and conduct of a study, hasty preplanned analysis is false economy at best and, at worst, risks gross misrepresentation of the data.

Most importantly, the researcher is not simply choosing a "test" to confirm some hypothesis. He is, or should be, investigating the heuristic value of alternative statistical representations of his data. As J. W. Tukey (1969, p. 90) notes:

Data analysis needs to be both exploratory and confirmatory. In exploratory data analysis there can be no substitute for flexibility, for adapting what is calculated—and, we hope, plotted—both to the needs of the situation and the clues that the data have already provided. In this mode, data analysis is detective work—almost an ideal example of seeking what might be relevant.

With this view, we planned to reanalyze the RJ data as a case study.

Reanalysis

Our reanalysis had two major objectives: 1) to provide a critical appraisal of the analytic approach taken by RJ and the conclusions warranted by the RJ data, 2) to discuss and illustrate the options available for exploring data of this type and the problems likely to be encountered with alternative approaches.

In a complex unbalanced design with measurement problems, there is no one best way to analyze the data and the results may look rather different from one method of analysis to another. It would, in general, be preferable to analyze such data in several ways and compare the results. With imperfect data, potential problems associated with the application of particular methods may sometimes be balanced by comparing the results obtained from each. If the results are consistent across methods of analysis, we can feel more secure about our conclusions. If not, the selection of which analysis is really most appropriate is crucial to the final conclusions. Choices must be made carefully and reasoning must be made explicit. As our work proceeded, it became clear how crucial to the choice of analysis in the RJ study were the issues, raised earlier, of unbalanced sampling plan, 20% subject loss, and the measurement problems of extreme scores and unreliability. The complete reanalysis is presented in Appendix A.

The Pygmalion Effect

Our reanalysis reveals no treatment effect or "expectancy advantage" in grades 3 through 6. The first and second graders may or may not exhibit some expectancy effect; these experimental and control groups differ greatly on the pretest and a statistical analysis of such data cannot provide clear conclusions. There is enough suggestion of an expectancy effect in <u>grades 1 and 2</u> to warrant further research, but the RJ experiment certainly does not demonstrate the existence of an expectancy effect or indicate what its size may be.

Chapter VI by J. Philip Baker and Janet Crist reviews the findings of recent investigations of teacher expectancy.

Recommendations for Further Research

As an aid to planning further research on teacher expectancy effects, as well as a summary of the present report, we offer here a brief review of general recommendations for the conduct of research.

1) As a first step in planning research, state as clearly as possible the proposition under study. This statement should suggest immediately what the key features of the research design are to be. Comparison of proposition and plan will show if questions other than the stated one are implied by the design. For example, RJ (p. 61)† stated that their experiment " . . . was designed specifically to test the proposition that within a given classroom those children from whom the teacher expected greater intellectual growth would show such greater growth." However, RJ did not really plan their primary analyses to be conducted "within classrooms" and never asked the teachers to indicate "those children from whom they expected greater intellectual growth."

2) Define as clearly as possible the psychological construct being measured. Avoid questionable connotations in naming variables. Consider in detail the scale of measurement, the reliability, and the construct validity of the measures chosen, whether they represent independent or dependent variables. Provide at least two separate measures of all constructs of primary interest in the experiment and examine the extent to which the data support or qualify the original formulation of the construct in question. RJ frequently used terms like "intellectual growth" and "expectancy advantage" in referring to their dependent variable, never discussing the possibility that their simple IQ gain score might not represent the construct of interest to them. RJ offered no information about raw scores or mental ages on their single instrument and made no direct use of other intellectual measures, some of which must have been available from school records. "Intellectual growth" must mean more than changing a few answers the second time through a single test. Neither the reliability nor the validity issues involved in this measure were fully explicated or studied. The term "expectancy advantage" also presumes interpretations before effects are found, a practice especially to be condemned in publications like *Pygmalion* which are aimed directly at the lay public.

Words like "special" and "magic" are frequently used by RJ to refer to experimental children, when less imaginative words would serve as well.

3) Specify as clearly as possible the population to which generalization is planned. Spell out in detail the steps involved in the sampling plan. Where alternative procedures for sampling or assigning subjects to experimental conditions exists, or where subjects are excluded from the analysis, summarize the reasoning that led to the decisions made. After producing a preliminary design, list all possible alternative interpretations for alternative expected results. Modify or expand the design to eliminate competing and confounding hypotheses and clarify in simple terms the outcomes expected and the implications of each outcome for the hypothesis of interest. Avoid unnecessarily complex designs and the addition of variables of marginal relevance. The final sampling plan and design should provide clear balance with respect to the main comparisons planned. RJ actually said little about the sampling plan. The need for balancing and the effect of its loss were not made clear. The reader was left uncertain regarding many points of concern regarding subject loss, transfer and balancing, and the effects of these issues on the results.

4) Validate the experimental treatment by providing checks and observations to ascertain that treatments really represent for the subjects what they were planned to represent for the experimenters. Observe and describe subject behavior in test administration conditions as well as in experimental treatment conditions. RJ could have included observations of teachers and students during tests and teaching but chose not to do so. The teacher interview, on the other hand, was a useful addition. It showed, however, that RJ's teachers could not remember, and perhaps had never known, who the "bloomers" were in the first place.

5) Look carefully at the basic raw data, before applying complex scoring formulae, transformations, or summarizations. Plot all relationships of interest graphically. One picture is worth many summary numbers. Use simple statistical computations to probe the assumptions and adequacy of more complex statistical abstractions. The most appropriate and productive mental set for the experimenter is that of a detective, not a defense attorney. Analyze the data in several alternative ways. RJ gave no evidence of having looked at raw data, scatterplotted relations, or of having probed into the structure of their analyses. Alternative methods of analysis were not discussed and the adequacy of the methods chosen was not questioned.

6) Emphasize the strength and character of relationships. Avoid

reducing continuous variables to dichotomous conceptualizations and decisions. Consider the amount of criterion variance accounted for in a relation at least as important as its statistical significance. Report *p*-values within any predetermined limits, but interpret no relation unless *p* is less than a fixed value such as .05. Report *p*-values less than .01 as "< .01." RJ relied almost completely on significance tests to characterize the importance of their findings and wrongly used *p*-value as a measure of strength of effect to indicate size and practical significance of mean differences. Nominal *p*-values ranging from .25 to .00002 were quoted throughout their work.

7) Use the full power of the data to reach simple rather than complex conclusions, whenever the former account for the data. The form of analysis chosen by RJ led them into unnecessarily complex results. Forming gain scores does not use the power of the data; using IQ instead of raw scores adds to complexity. Treating the four test occasions in separate analyses ignores the powerful repeated measures aspect of the data. Analyzing reasoning, verbal, and total scores separately also adds to complexity, since the latter is a simple summation and thus is literally dependent upon the first two subscores. RJ conducted many separate analyses without attempting to show the full set of possible comparisons or to use interrelationships among variables for data reduction. Their unweighted means analysis is a gross approximation to least squares solutions at best, especially when proportional cell sizes were expressly built into the experiment.

8) Report the results of research as fully and as clearly as possible, using appendices and supplementary publication where necessary. Use scientific and professional journals as the initial outlet for research findings, paying conscientious attention to the suggestions and criticisms of referees and reviewers. Single unreplicated studies of broad public concern should be incorporated into popular books only with due regard for the degree of their possible substantiation by other research and their possible misinterpretation by the public.

The educational researcher will deal increasingly with hypotheses and conclusions of far-reaching social importance. While researchers are always responsible for the proper conduct and reporting of research, nowhere should this responsibility be more keenly felt and exercised than in work bearing directly on urgent and volatile social issues. It is essential, then, that both researchers and publishers recognize this responsibility and pursue it to the utmost. It is hoped that this report will help to equip future workers for that pursuit.

Teacher Expectancies: A Review of the Literature

*J. Philip Baker
and Janet L. Crist*

In earlier chapters the RJ methodology was shown to be sufficiently faulty to throw doubt on the teacher expectancy effects RJ claimed to have shown. It was concluded that the study provided some suggestive evidence of a teacher expectancy effect but that replication of the study was the only way to reach any firm conclusions about the existence and extent of teacher expectancy effects.

The purpose of this chapter is to review the research pertinent to investigation of teacher expectancy, with primary emphasis on attempts at replicating the RJ study. No serious attempt has been made to evaluate the methodology of the research papers summarized in this chapter. The amount of work involved in a careful review of the methodology of each paper would be prohibitive. The reader should keep in mind that a number of the studies reviewed here may be subject to the same methodological criticisms as the RJ study; indeed, some of the papers contain methodological flaws obvious at first reading. Unfortunately, to ascertain whether correction of flaws in the methodology would result in changes in the reported findings would require examination of the raw data.

Direct Attempts
at Replication

The nine studies immediately following represent attempts to replicate the RJ finding. The experiments reported vary in the degree to which the RJ procedure was followed. We have tried to summarize the essential features and results of each study without reproducing them at length. For questions about details, readers should refer to the original reports.

W. L. Claiborn (1969) used 12 first grade classrooms, since the RJ results seemed most significant in the lower grades. The RJ expectancy induction was given in the spring and post measures taken two months later. The criterion measures were IQ gain (using TOGA) and observations of teacher-pupil interactions in the classroom. No significant expectancy effects were found on any of the variables. However, the time of expectancy induction and the length of the experiment differed from the RJ study. RJ induced expectancies at the beginning of the school year while Claiborn induced expectancies one month into the spring term. Thus a previous semester of teacher-pupil interaction provided a background of experience with each child before the bogus expectancy was introduced, and the expectancy variable was in effect only two months; it is probable that teachers' impressions and expectancies concerning pupils were already well formed and not easily changed during the spring term. Claiborn also attempted to show effects on observed teacher behavior, without success. He reported that teachers in his study recalled the names of the special pupils with considerably more accuracy than did teachers in the RJ study. Of course, the names might have been "fresher" in the minds of teachers in the Claiborn study.

J. José (1971) used first and second grade classrooms; four experimental and four control students were randomly selected from each of 18 classrooms. Expectancy induction apparently occurred during the first month of the spring term; post measures of IQ gain (TOGA), changes in reading and arithmetic subtests of the Metropolitan Achievement Tests (MAT), and teacher-pupil interaction were obtained 16 weeks later. No significant differences were found between the experimental and control pupils on any of the criterion measures. The author reported that expectancy induction apparently failed for the majority of teachers in her study, and suggested that the means of establishing expectancy was crucial to the success of future studies. José suggested that simply giving IQ information to teachers may not be sufficient to establish the desired expectancy since teacher expectancies are influenced by so many additional factors in the natural situation. Her results indicate that the failure to find expectancy effects in other studies may be due to the failure of expectancy induction.

J. T. Evans and R. Rosenthal (1969) performed a partial replication in a middle-class elementary school in the Midwest, using first through sixth grade pupils. There was no expectancy main effect; an interaction effect was found for Reasoning IQ. Girl "bloomers" gained less than girl nonbloomers, and boy "bloomers" gained more than boy nonbloomers—just the reverse of RJ's results.

A study by L. Conn, C. Edwards, R. Rosenthal, and D. Crowne (1968) attempted to investigate the underlying process of expectancy effects, using 258 first through sixth graders in a middle-class suburban school. The usual RJ expectancy induction was given in February, and post measures of IQ (TOGA) were taken four months later. Again, IQ gain served as the dependent variable. A measure of student accuracy in perceiving vocally expressed emotion was also obtained. There were no clear expectancy effects, but results showed that accurate perception of female communication of emotion was associated with significantly greater gains in IQ (TOGA) for "special" children, especially for boys. The authors suggested that "an important factor in the interaction process is an ability to perceive and interpret accurately subtle, nonverbal communications of emotion, communications quite independent of actual content." (p. 33)

E. S. Fleming and R. G. Anttonen (1971 a and b) investigated the effect of different expectancy conditions on learner achievement, self-concept, and teacher grading behavior on approximately 900 second grade students. In the fall, teachers were given one of four items of information about each pupil: 1) Kuhlmann-Anderson IQ inflated by 16 points, 2) actual IQ, 3) actual PMA percentiles (Primary Mental Abilities), or 4) no information. Within each classroom, pupils were assigned at random to one of the four conditions. Criterion measures (IQ, SAT, and self-concept) were taken in February and again in the spring. Teachers were also given a questionnaire assessing opinions toward tests in general.

There were no significant expectancy effects revealed in the IQ or self-concept measures. One subtest of the SAT showed a significant effect in February, but not in the spring. There was, however, a significant teacher opinion effect; teachers who held tests in high regard had classes showing higher IQ's and higher scores on the SAT reading and arithmetic subtests in the spring. These teachers also gave higher average grades in all subject areas. In addition, an interaction of SES with teacher opinion toward tests was noted; low opinion teachers discriminated more between two SES groups in assigning grades than did the high opinion teachers. Most of the student measures also showed an SES x opinion interaction, but the pattern was not consistent. The variables of SES and teacher opinion toward tests were apparently more powerful influencers of teacher behavior than the artificial induction procedures.

J. S. Goldsmith and E. Fry (1970) used 112 experimental and 112 control students in a high school. Expectancy lists were given to teachers in September and post measures taken five months later. The criterion measures were gains in IQ (TOGA) and gains in scores on the Sequential Tests of Educational Progress (STEP-2B). In addition, the teachers were reminded of the list of bloomers from three to five times during the following five months. A follow-up questionnaire confirmed expectancy induction in only 29 of 61 teachers returning the questionnaire. There were no significant expectancy effects on TOGA or STEP-2B.

D. F. Anderson and R. Rosenthal (1968) reported a partial replication using a much shortened time span and multiple teacher contacts with subjects. Subjects were 28 institutionalized retarded boys (ages 9-16); their summer day camp counselors were given the bogus expectancy after a TOGA pretest. During the following eight weeks, the amount of attention paid by the counselors to the boys was observed. Then, TOGA and a measure of Self-Help were administered as posttests. There was no significant change in IQ as a result of the expectancy treatment. It was found that the counselors paid less attention to the "bloomers" and that the "bloomers" gained more in Self-Help. It is not known whether the boys became more independent because they had less attention, or whether they required less attention because of some other mediating mechanism.

RJ (p. 58) reviewed an earlier study by C. F. Flowers (1966) which showed inconsistent expectancy effects on IQ and achievement, but which revealed more positive teacher attitudes towards the "high" groups.

S. Kester (1971) investigated teacher-pupil interaction in seventh grade classrooms. There were 23 teachers and 150 average ability students; the latter were randomly assigned to experimental and control groups. Teachers were given the names of "bright" students in their classes during the first week of school in the fall and told that these students would be observed as part of a study on classroom behavior of bright students. Teacher interaction with experimental and control students was observed during the following seven weeks to determine positive interactions directed to the student, verbal praise, and nonverbal positive behavior. The Stanford Achievement Test (SAT), an IQ test (Otis-Lennon), and an attitude scale were used as pupil pretests and posttests during the first and ninth weeks of school. There were no significant expectancy effects on the pupil measures. Teachers did appear to display more "supportive" behavior toward "bright" students; they talked to them more and spent more time particularly with "bright" students who returned positive behaviors to the teacher.

The nine studies summarized above each represent unsuccessful attempts at replication of the RJ results. In none of the studies was IQ significantly altered by expectancy. None of the studies showed significant expectancy effects on pupil performance measures. A major problem seems to be that of determining whether expectancy induction has in fact occurred. It seems doubtful that a list of pupil names representing expected "bloomers" is sufficient to cause changes in basic measures like IQ through the subtle medium of teacher expectations.

It must be noted that none of these studies replicated RJ exactly, but varied from the RJ paradigm in time or method of inductancy, length of experimental conditions, or age and grade of subjects. Six of these studies examined teacher and/or pupil behavior, and "expectancy effects" appeared in differential classroom or social behavior in pupils and/or teachers in four of the six studies. Other variables which appear important for future investigations are teacher opinion of tests, student SES, and student accuracy in perceiving vocally expressed emotion.

Related Studies

While the Pygmalion effect as described by RJ has not been replicated, it has stimulated significant studies. Many additional studies related to the phenomenon of teacher expectancies have been conducted, some focusing on the teacher, some on the learner, and some on teacher-pupil interaction.

Studies of the Teacher

The three studies reviewed here deal with the effects of expectations on the teacher as perceiver. M. Haberman (1970) used 120 student teachers (STs) and their cooperating teachers (CTs), manipulating expectancies for both groups by dividing them into four conditions: STs who were told they had an outstanding CT; CTs who were told their STs had high potential; both STs and CTs given high expectations for their counterparts; and a control group in which neither STs nor CTs were given particular expectations. At the end of the term of student teaching, no significant differences were found among the conditions on either STs' ratings of their CTs or CTs' ratings of STs. The author suggested that STs and CTs may have had such clearly defined objectives in this situation that their perceptions of each other were not susceptible to the influence attempted.

Two studies manipulated expectancies about hypothetical or absent pupils unknown to the college student subjects asked to score pieces of the pupils' work. L. S. Cahen (1966) found a significant expectancy effect on subjective scores given by 256 teachers-in-training on a learning readiness test, when fictitious information was supplied about pupils' IQ and reading group placement. Teachers gave higher scores to allegedly "bright" pupils than they did to allegedly "dull" pupils.

W. E. Simon (1969) also found that scorers (college students) who were told their twelve-year-old subjects were above average gave significantly higher scores on 20 items taken from the middle half of the vocabulary subtest of the Wechsler Intelligence Scale for Children (WISC) than scorers who were told their subjects were below average. Test protocols of real subjects (all in the average IQ range) were used, but the ability labels were assigned randomly.

Two of the preceding three studies showed expectancy effects on teachers' perceptions of pupils and the operation of a halo effect (see W. J. Gephart and D. P. Antonopolos, 1969) resulting in a differential grading according to an induced expectancy set.

Studies of the Learner

The following six studies investigated effects of either manipulated or existing teacher expectations upon measures of pupils' achievement or sociometric ratings.

D. H. Meichenbaum, K. S. Bowers, and R. R. Ross (1969) used 14 female adolescent juvenile offenders as subjects with 6 girls classified as "bloomers." The design differed from RJ in several ways: TOGA was *not* given because the experimental period available to the experimenters was too short (two weeks) to expect changes in IQ; criterion measures were objective and subjective exam scores given by the teachers. The four teachers were all given the same induction and all taught all of the girls. Teachers were observed and rated on positive, negative, and neutral interactions with pupils during the two-week experimental period. The girls were rated on class-appropriate behavior. A significant expectancy effect appeared on the girls' objective exam measure and class-appropriate behavior, but not on subjective grades. Before the experiment began, teachers were asked to identify the "good" and "poor" pupils in their classes. Three "good" pupils and three "poor" pupils were then selected as "late bloomers," supposedly on the basis of tests administered earlier. The teachers all agreed that the test was accurate in identifying the "good" students as "bloomers." Although initially surprised by the names of the "poor" students labeled as bloomers, the teachers were soon citing instances in the behavior of these girls that indicated they did indeed have intellectual potential.

The principal value of this study is the information it gives about the reactions of the different teachers to the expectancy instructions. There was a significant decrease in negative teacher behavior toward the "bloomers" and a significant teacher x expectancy group interaction for positive behavior. Analysis of individual teacher behavior suggested that 1) teachers react differently to expectancy induction, 2) prior expectancy also influences teacher behavior, and 3) student effects of expectancy conditions are not always related to teacher behavior we observe.

RJ (p. 57) reviewed a study by C. C. V. Pitt (1956) that found no expectancy effects on school grades, achievement tests, or teacher ratings. An effect on pupil self-ratings was obtained however.

J. M. Palardy (1969) studied existing teacher expectations about the probable success of boys, compared with girls, in learning to read. Forty-two first grade teachers returned questionnaires in December indicating their opinions. Five teachers who thought boys' probability of success was about equal to girls' (Group A) were matched (on the basis of race, experience, location of schools, and grouping and materials used in their classes) with five who believed boys' probability of success was lower (Group B). Reading achievement of 107 pupils (53 boys, 54 girls) of Group A teachers and 109 pupils (58 boys, 51 girls) of Group B teachers was measured in May (Stanford Achievement Test, Primary Battery, Form X). Pretests in September had shown no significant differences in scores between students in these groups. The results in May, with IQ as a covariate, showed that boys with Group B teachers scored considerably lower in reading achievement than girls of either group and boys of Group A. This finding suggests the possibility of differential reading achievement according to expectancies developed naturally by teachers. It is unfortunate that the matching procedure apparently excluded so many teachers from the sample. A more complete analysis would have been informative.

Two reports by W. R. Schrank (1968,1970) may be considered as experimental and control conditions of a single study. In each, the students taking a college freshman mathematics course were randomly divided into class sections according to five simulated ability groupings. In the first study, the instructors did not know that class assignment for the 100 students in five sections had actually been made randomly rather than according to ability (ability grouping was the usual practice for these classes); in the second experiment with 420 students, instructors were told that class assignment was random. The report does not specify how many sections were used in the later study. Criterion measures were test and course grades. For the first year, the highest and lowest labeled sections differed significantly on all test and course grade comparisons. The five sections were almost perfectly ordered on criterion averages and labeled ability, from highest to lowest. In the second study, few significant differences between pairs of higher and lower labeled groups were found. No actual data were given for either study, and one can question the reported use of a large series of *t*-tests as the sole statistical analysis. However, an expectancy effect deserving of further attention is suggested by the results.

Jacobs (1970) investigated expectancy effects on sociometric factors. After preliminary sociometric analysis of all 14 classrooms in an elementary school, he gave teachers bogus information about 20% of the children who were designated as potential sociometric "stars." The time of the expectancy induction was not stated, but apparently it was not at the beginning of the year. There was a positive correlation between teachers' *post hoc* ratings of sociometric change in the classrooms and actual measured change, indicating that teachers were sensitive to small changes of social structure in their rooms. But post treatment sociometric ratings (10 weeks later) showed no changes in peer acceptance of the experimental group members.

W. B. Seaver (1971) used archival data to investigate the effects of natural expectancy inductions. He reported two analyses of school records for elementary school children in an upper-middle-class suburb of Chicago. The first, which included data on 80 pupils entering grade 5, was a lagged correlational study using fall IQ scores (Primary Mental Abilities) in grade 1 to predict midyear grade point averages in grades 1, 2, 3, and 4, and then these GPAs to predict IQ scores in the fall of grade 4. He reasoned that if IQ scores influence teacher expectations about student performance and thus influence performance, correlations of grade 1 IQ with GPA in grades 1-4 should be higher than correlations of GPA in grades 1-4 with IQ in grade 4. The results of this analysis were uninterpretable, however, because of nonstationarity of the variables, probably due to relatively lower reliability of the IQ measure in grade 1.

Seaver also investigated a possible expectancy effect due to a teacher's prior experience in teaching a pupil's older sibling. From records of two elementary schools, 79 pairs of siblings were identified and separated according to whether or not the same or a different teacher had taught both siblings. Then, the older siblings were separated by independent judges into "good" or "bad" categories on the basis of their first grade IQ, Stanford Achievement Test scores, and grade point average. Within this four-fold classification, younger siblings were then compared using six Stanford Achievement Test subtests and grade point average for grade 1. Four of the subtests showed significant interaction; younger siblings of good students obtained higher achievement scores if assigned to their sibling's teacher than if assigned to a different teacher. Younger siblings of poor students did better with new teachers than their peers did with the teachers who had had their older siblings. The general form of this interaction is illustrated in the following figure.

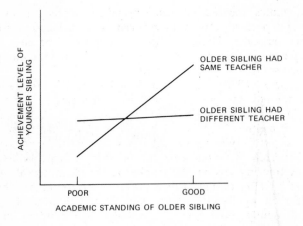

The Seaver study is important because it clearly illustrates expectancy effects in a natural situation, without contrived experimental conditions or deceptions of uncertain validity. With archival data of this sort, the influence of both positive and negative expectancies can be examined; the ethics of producing negative expectancies experimentally would be questionable. It is hoped that future studies will follow Seaver's lead and probe data of this sort further. One issue deserving attention is whether the older siblings' academic standing established the expectancy directly, or whether teachers are attending primarily to disruptiveness and other classroom behavior only correlated with scholastic measures. Another concern is whether the teacher was instrumental at all, since self-fulfilling prophecies could have been brought from home by the younger siblings. Still another question for future work concerns the amount of teacher experience with the younger sibling that is necessary to reduce the effects of prior expectations. Seaver studied grade 1 achievement; a similar examination of later grade records could be enlightening.

To summarize this group of six studies (viewing the two Schrank reports as one experiment), two of the four studies using bogus expectancies showed expectancy effects on student achievement, while both of the studies utilizing existing or natural expectancies did so. The one study with a sociometric criterion measure did not show expectancy effects; the expectancy condition was weakest here, having been introduced after teachers had had ample opportunity to form impressions of their pupils.

Studies on Teacher-Pupil Interaction

Seven studies focused on teacher-student interaction as the measure of expectancy effects, though some also included measures of learner outcome. These studies are important because they begin to focus upon the dynamics of expectancies and the interpersonal processes that may serve as media.

W. V. Beez (1970) followed a design in which 60 graduate students tutored 60 preschool children, teaching a series of symbols in a 15-minute session. Teachers were led to believe their "pupils" were either "high" or "low" in ability, though labels were actually assigned randomly (actual IQs were not obtained for the study). Criterion measures were the number of symbols learned during the tutoring session, the number tutors attempted to teach, and tutors' *post hoc* ratings of their tutees. It was found that "high" pupils learned significantly more symbols and their tutors gave them consistently more favorable ratings than children in the "low" labeled group. On the surface, this experiment seems to support the expectancy hypothesis. But tutoring differs conceptually from classroom teaching, where general instructional conditions are common to both "bloomers" and nonbloomers. A tutor meeting a "high" ability pupil *should* plan to teach more, and 15 minutes hardly allows interaction sufficient for ratings. Such superficial ratings probably indicate only that the tutors understood the experimenter's expectancy.

W. E. Brown (1970) investigated the effects on teacher behavior of fake psychological reports, containing information on intelligence, SES, and personality such as is often found in students' cumulative records. The experiment used 10 teacher trainees to tutor 80 first graders on a paired-associate list of states and their capital cities. As in the Beez (1970) study, bogus IQ information was related to the number of pairs the teachers attempted to teach. However, the effect on expectancy-fulfillment ratings of teachers was opposite to that predicted from the expectancy hypothesis. SES and personality information had no relation to criterion measures.*

---

*Review summarized from *Dissertation Abstracts*. The dissertation was not read.

P. Rubovits and M. Maehr (1970) investigated the expectancy effect on teacher behavior in a microteaching situation. Teachers were 26 female undergraduates; students were 104 sixth and seventh graders. The expectancy induction was accomplished by giving the teacher a seating chart for the four students used in her microteaching session. The chart included randomly assigned IQs and "gifted" or "regular" labels for each student. Teachers were rated on the amount of praise, encouragement, elaboration, ignoring, and criticism used during the session; a dogmatism scale was also administered. Teachers were found to request significantly more statements from, and to give significantly more praise to, the "gifted" students although there was no difference in the total amount of attention paid to either group. The attention patterns used with the regular group were not specified. There was no effect related to teacher dogmatism.

M. Rothbart et al. (1971) investigated teacher-pupil interaction in microteaching, using 13 female undergraduates and 52 high school students in a 30-minute literature discussion. There were positive *and negative* expectancies induced in this experiment; two of four students in each microteaching group were labeled as having greater academic potential, two were described as lacking in potential. Teachers were observed to spend somewhat more time attending to "bright" students, and these students tended to talk more. Differences only approached significance, however ($p < .06$ in both cases). There was no difference in the amount of reinforcement given to each student. On *post hoc* ratings of the students, teachers described bright students as significantly more likely to have greater future success and as needing less approval.

B. J. Willis (1970) asked each of five teachers of special classes to rank their eight students from most efficient (ME) to least efficient as learners (LE). The top and bottom students in each class, along with their teachers, were then observed in simulated classroom sessions 30 minutes a day for eight days. Measures of teacher-pupil interaction showed teachers ignoring LE comments more frequently than ME comments and providing more verbal responses to ME comments than to LE comments. The observed "child behavior-teacher reaction" sequences were different for ME and LE students; the author concluded that " . . . the teachers provided consequences for the behavior of the LE which might be described as systematic extinction of the behavior the LE most needs to develop for social competence."*

A study by T. L. Good (1970) in four first grade classrooms sought to assess opportunities given by the teacher for pupils to

---

*Review summarized from *Dissertation Abstracts*. The dissertation was not read. Quote is from the abstract.

respond in class. The teacher's own ranking of her pupils according to her assessment of their achievement served as a measure of existing expectations. Two days of observations in each classroom determined the number of opportunities given each child to respond as a function of his achievement ranking—high, middle, or low. Significant differences were found among the three groups of pupils, favoring the high achievers. Opportunities varied somewhat from class to class, but high achievers consistently received many more response opportunities. Low achievers received far fewer opportunities in all classes but one (in which they tied the middle ranked group). Thus, differential interaction patterns between teachers and pupils were substantially related to teachers' earlier ratings of pupils' achievement.

J. Brophy and Good (1970) followed the design of Good's earlier study, again using teachers' rankings of achievement to measure expectations for pupils' classroom performance. Six pupils (three boys and three girls) were selected from high and low ends of the achievement rankings for each of four first-grade teachers. Observers rated teacher-child interactions on four separate days for the 12 pupils in each class. It was found that high achievers initiated significantly more contacts with their teachers than did low achievers, but that the total number of teacher-afforded response opportunities did not differ significantly between the two groups of pupils. A difference in quality (as opposed to quantity) in the total pattern of dyadic contacts was noted, however. Significant differences were found for all dependent variables assessing pupils' quality of academic performance favoring the high achievers. The most important results concerned teacher differences in eliciting and reinforcing of performance in the high and low pupils. The authors summarize their findings:

The data show that the teachers consistently favored the highs over the lows in demanding and reinforcing quality performance. Despite the fact that the highs gave more correct answers and fewer incorrect answers than did the lows, they were more frequently praised when correct, and less frequently criticized when incorrect or unable to respond. Furthermore, the teachers were more persistent in eliciting responses from the highs then (*sic*) they were with the lows . . . the teachers failed to give any feedback whatever only 3.33% of the time when reacting to highs, while the corresponding figure for lows is 14.75%, a highly significant difference.(p. 372)

As supporting illustration for the findings of Good (1970), Brophy and Good (1970), and Willis (1970), anthropological observations by R.C. Rist (1970) provide striking anecdotes about teachers' differential treatments of differently judged children. He followed a class of black ghetto children from kindergarten

Summary of Studies Reviewed

Study	Type and Strength of Treatment	Teacher Behavior	Expectancy Effect* on Pupil Behavior				
			In Class	Achievement Post	Achievement Gain	IQ Post	IQ Gain
Replication Attempts							
Claiborn (1969)	weak induced	0					0
José (1971)	weak induced	0	0		0		0
Evans and Rosenthal (1968)	weak induced						0
Conn, et al (1968)	weak induced						0
Fleming and Anttonen (1971a,b)	weak induced	+		0		0	
Goldsmith and Fry (1970)	moderate induced				0		0
Anderson and Rosenthal (1968)	weak induced	+	+				0
Flowers (1966)	strong induced	+		0			0
Kester (1971)	weak induced	+			0		0
Related Studies							
Haberman (1970)	weak induced	0	0				
Cahen (1966)	weak induced	+					
Simon (1969)	weak induced	+					
Meichenbaum, et al (1969)	strong induced	+	+	+			
Pitt (1956)	weak induced			0			
Palardy (1969)	strong natural			+			
Schrank (1968, 1970)	moderate induced			+			
Jacobs (1970)	weak induced		0				
Seaver (1971)	strong natural			+			
Beez (1970)	moderate induced	+		+			
Brown (1970)	moderate induced	+					
Rubovits and Maehr (1970)	moderate induced	+					
Rothbart, et al (1971)	moderate induced	+	0				
Willis (1970)	strong natural	+					
Good (1970)	strong natural	+					
Brophy and Good (1970)	strong natural	+	+	+			

*Results: + = significant expectancy effects obtained; 0 = no significant effects or differences obtained; blank = not applicable.

through the second grade. He notes information available to the teacher about home, family, and SES, obtained by parent interview, and about pupil appearance and performance during the first few days of school. Later assignments of children to tables and classroom tasks as well as the general quality of teacher interaction showed clear discrimination between groups of favored and nonfavored children in the room. The initial groupings and differential treatment were shown to persist through three grade levels.

Three of these studies illustrate a planning effect in tutoring situations as the result of bogus expectancy induction. One illustrates the effect of the self-fulfilling prophecy on student behavior, and three more demonstrate how teachers' ratings of students according to achievement or ability relate to teacher treatment of pupils. All the studies which measured pupil behavior as well showed expectancy effects on this criterion. Two of four show the effect on pupil achievement where it was included in the design.

Summary and Theoretical Overview

The table on page 60 provides a summary of the studies reviewed above in terms of the type of expectancy used (induced or natural), an assessment of the strength of the expectancy in operation, and the results for each type of criterion measure (IQ, academic, teacher behavior, or pupil behavior).

From the summary table and preceding discussion, the following generalizations and recommendations seem warranted:

1. Teacher expectancy probably does not affect pupil IQ. This conclusion is supported by a background of decades of research suggesting the stability of human intelligence and its resistance to alterations by environmental manipulation, by the reanalysis of RJ reported earlier in this book, and by the failure of all replication studies to demonstrate effects on IQ. RJ's conclusions can therefore not be justified. It is noted that all replication attempts used only weak or moderate induced expectancies. It is possible that strong, naturally occurring teacher expectancies could influence intellectual growth over an extended period of time. The issue remains a hypothesis for further research.

2. Teacher expectancy may affect pupil achievement. Significant effects are likely if a strong teacher expectancy exists naturally or if the induction is strong and a close simulation of natural conditions, but unlikely with weak induction procedures such as those used by RJ. Effects on achievement may be somewhat more likely on teacher-controlled achievement measures and

less likely on standardized achievement measures independent of specific material taught.

3. Teacher expectancy probably affects observable teacher and pupil behavior, if the expectancy condition occurs naturally or provides a moderate to strong manipulation of inducement. In manipulated situations where the establishment of expectancies was demonstrated with some certainty, effects occurred. Where there were no results to indicate the operation of expectancy effects, the inducement was likely ineffective in the first place. The teacher behavior most likely to be affected involves eliciting and reinforcing of children's responses, the kind of attention given to pupils, the amount of teaching actually attempted, subjective scoring or grading of pupil work, and judgments or ratings of pupil ability and probable success. The pupil behavior most likely to be affected involves the kind of response given to the teacher, the child's initiation of activity, his class-appropriate behavior, and his feelings about school, self, and teacher.

4. We recommend that the line of research following RJ's paradigm be abandoned in favor of the detailed examination of natural situations exemplified by the Seaver study. The dependent variables most worthy of study in such research will probably be measures of teacher-pupil interaction processes and teacher-controlled achievement. To examine interaction processes in detail, it may sometimes be advantageous to induce expectations experimentally. At such times, a strong positive inducement, simulating natural conditions, should be introduced before stable impressions have occurred naturally. Measures should be included to show that the treatment functioned as planned for each teacher and the analysis should take into account that individual teachers and pupils are likely to be affected differently by the treatment.

5. In pursuing research on expectancies in interpersonal interaction it should be advantageous to work within the theoretical frameworks provided by the person perception literature in social psychology. Five general guidelines are available from this literature.*

   a. People view others according to their own personality. Just as human beings generally, teachers view pupils in terms of their own values and needs. They may prefer quiet or exuberant pupils, have special empathy for disturbed children, identifying as successful those pupils who are most like

---

*We refer the reader who is unfamiliar with the person perception literature to Heider (1958); Tagiuri and Petrullo (1958); Secord and Backman (1964); Taguiri (1969); Freedman, Carlsmith, and Sears (1970); Guskin and Guskin (1970); Hastorf, Schneider, and Polefka (1970).

themselves. One teacher may evaluate pupils on cleanliness, another on discipline, while still another teacher may give primary value to creative production; teachers will thus have different views of the same pupils.

b. People form stable impressions on limited information. Like other human beings, teachers meeting pupils for the first time form impressions based on physical appearance and conduct. They may also know something about each pupil's past conduct, achievement, IQ scores, or the general character of older siblings or parents. These impressions based on a day's or a week's experience may produce expectations about pupil behavior and future achievement. Since these initial impressions are fairly stable, they may be expected to influence teacher-pupil interaction for the remainder of the year.

c. People form impressions in global terms. When teachers characterize pupils they are likely to label them as "good" or "bad." Clean children may be "good" and dirty ones "bad;" or there may be "fast" and "slow" learners. The tendency for these global classifications to affect other judgments is called a halo effect.

d. Information conflicting with current impressions may be rearranged to resolve contradictions. This tendency preserves the global images discussed above. It allows the perceiver to handle discrepant events without overhauling his over-all impressions and expectations about a person. If a "poor" student scores poorly on an exam, he "couldn't do any better;" if a "good" student scores poorly, he "had an off day." Global impressions once formed are not readily altered by contradictory information.

e. Interaction between perceiver and perceived may influence how the perceived subsequently presents himself. The human teacher's tendency to make new information consistent with existing impressions has its counterpart in the pupil's tendency to conform to expectations. The pupil may begin to act in a manner consistent with previous interactions with the teacher. It is this aspect of person perception theory that may represent the primary mechanism of self-fulfilling prophecy.

The reader should realize that the words "pupil" and "teacher" can be interchanged: the perceiver is also the perceived, and pupils are forming impressions and expectancies of teachers at the same time that teachers are coming to know the pupils. Perhaps the teacher also comes to conform to pupil expectations. The processes described here, while simple to state, occur as a complex stream of interpersonal transactions, each influencing both parties in further transactions.

The question for future research is not whether there are expectancy effects, but how they operate in school situations. Such research will need multivariate criterion measures, as well as a multivariate conception of the teacher and pupil susceptibilities that affect the operation of interpersonal expectancies in both directions. There is legitimate concern about the possible negative effects of teacher expectancy on some children. With further understanding of such processes growing from improved research, effective school administrative arrangements and teacher training programs could be developed to avert negative effects. The solutions eventually devised will hopefully capitalize on informed, humane teaching; they are not likely to include the withholding or misrepresenting of prior information about pupils.

VII

Reviews

Review of
Pygmalion in the Classroom

Robert L. Thorndike

The enterprise which represents the core of this document, and presumably the excuse for its publication, has received widespread advance publicity. In spite of anything I can say, I am sure it will become a classic—widely referred to and rarely examined critically. Alas, it is so defective technically that one can only regret that it ever got beyond the eyes of the original investigators! Though the volume may be an effective addition to educational propagandizing, it does nothing to raise the standards of educational research.

Though it may make for a dull review, I feel I must dissect the study to point out some basic defects in its data that make its conclusions (though they may possibly be true) in no sense adequately supported by the data. The general reasonableness of the "self-fulfilling prophecy effect" is not at issue, nor is the reported background of previous anecdote, observation, and research. The one point at which this review is directed is the adequacy of procedures (of data gathering and data analysis) and the appropriateness of the conclusions drawn from the study that constitutes the middle third of the book.

Before we can dig beneath the surface, we must outline briefly on a surface level what was done and what was reportedly found. In May 1964, the SRA-published Tests of General Ability (TOGA) were administered by the classroom teachers to all pupils in kindergarten and all six grades of a school. The test had been presented to the teachers as a test that ". . . will allow us to

Reprinted from *American Educational Research Journal, 5* (1968), 708-711, by permission of the American Educational Research Association. Mr. Thorndike is associated with the Teachers College, Columbia University.

predict which youngsters are most likely to show an academic spurt." The following September each teacher was given a list of names of pupils (actually selected by a table of random numbers) who were alleged to be the ones likely to show a spurt.

The children were tested again in January 1965, May 1965, and May 1966. The authors assert that the results support the proposition that the teachers' expectancies influenced the mental development of the children.

The main results of testing in May 1965 (from the authors' Table 7-1) are as follows:

	Control			*Experimental*		
Grade	*N*	*Gain*		*N*	*Gain*	*Difference*
1	48	+12.0		7	+27.4	15.4
2	47	+ 7.0		12	+16.5	9.5
3	40	+ 5.0		14	+ 5.0	0
4	49	+ 2.2		12	+ 5.6	3.4
5	26	+17.5		9	+17.4	-0.1
6	45	+10.7		11	+10.0	-0.7

Thus, to all intents and purposes, the alleged effect of the "prophecy" appears in 19 children in grades 1 and 2. If we are to trust the results, and the large edifice of further analysis and speculation built upon them, the findings for these two grades must be unimpeachable. Let us examine them.

TOGA has two subtests, one consisting of oral vocabulary and one of multi-mental ("which one doesn't belong") items. For the K-2 level of the test, the one used in the pretesting and posttesting of grades 1 and 2, the two parts of the test contain respectively 35 and 28 items. Let us look first at the pretest data for six classrooms, three tested in kindergarten and three in the first grade. The results, from Appendix Tables A-2 and A-3 were (expressed in numbers that are always spoken of by the authors as "IQs"):

		Experimental			*Control*	
Class	*N*	*Mean Verbal "IQ"*	*Mean Reasoning "IQ"*	*N*	*Mean Verbal "IQ"*	*Mean Reasoning "IQ"*
1A	3	102.00	84.67	19	119.47	91.32
1B	4	116.25	54.00	16	104.25	47.19
1C	2	67.50	53.50	19	95.68	30.79
2A	6	114.33	112.50	19	111.53	100.95
2B	3	103.67	102.33	16	96.50	80.56
2C	5	90.20	77.40	14	82.21	73.93

On the Reasoning Test, one class of 19 pupils is reported to have a mean "IQ" of 31! They just barely appear to make the grade as imbeciles! And yet these pretest data were used blithely by the authors without even a reference to these fantastic results!

If these pretest data show anything, they show that the testing was utterly worthless and meaningless. The means and standard deviations for the total first and second grade classes were (calculated by combining sub-groups):

	First Grade		Second Grade	
	Mean	S. D.	Mean	S.D.
Verbal	105.7	21.2	99.4	16.1
Reasoning	58.0	36.8	89.1	21.6

What kind of a test, or what kind of testing is it that gives a mean "IQ" of 58 for the total entering first grade of a rather run-of-the-mill school?

Unfortunately, nowhere in the whole volume do the authors give any data expressed in raw scores. Neither do they give the ages of their groups. So it takes a little impressionistic estimating to try to reconstruct the picture. However, it would not be far off to assume an average age of 6.0 for May of a kindergarten year. An "IQ" of 58 would then mean a "mental age" of 3.5. So we go to the norms tables of TOGA to find the raw score that would correspond to a "mental age" of 3.5. Alas, the norms do not go down that far! It is not possible to tell what the authors did, but finding that a raw score of 8 corresponds to an "M.A." of 5.3, we can take a shot at extrapolating downward. We come out with a raw score of approximately 2! Random marking would give 5 or 6 right!

We can only conclude that the pretest on the so-called Reasoning Test at this age is worthless. And, in the words of a European colleague, "When the clock strikes thirteen, doubt is cast not only on the last stroke but also on all that have gone before."

Another look at one of the Appendix tables (A-6) shows that the 6 pupils in class 2A who had been picked to be "spurters" have a reported mean and standard deviation of posttest "IQ" of 150.17 and 40.17 respectively. This looks a little high! What does it mean in raw score terms? Again, we must turn detective with somewhat inadequate clues. Not knowing pupil ages, let us assume 7½ as probably on the low side for May in the second grade. An "IQ" of 150 implies, then, a mean "M.A." of 11¼. Back to our TOGA norms to find the corresponding raw score. Alas, the highest entry is 10.0 for a raw score of 26! We must once more extrapolate, and the best we can do from the existing data is to get 28 + . (Remember, there are only 28 items in this sub-test.) The mean of

6 represents a perfect score! But the standard deviation is 40 "IQ" points. What of those who fall above the mean?

When the clock strikes 14, we throw away the clock!

In conclusion, then, the indications are that the basic data upon which this structure has been raised are so untrustworthy that any conclusions based upon them must be suspect. The conclusions may be correct, but if so it must be considered a fortunate coincidence.

Empirical vs. Decreed Validation of Clocks and Tests

Robert Rosenthal

In his recent review of *Pygmalion in the Classroom* (Rosenthal and Jacobson, 1968) Thorndike (1968) raises such important questions about our research instrument and our results that answers to these questions must be made available.

At the beginning of the substantive portion of his review, the reviewer reported the results showing that the effects of favorable teacher expectations occurred only in the first two grades as measured by gains in total IQ. To show that none of the data need be taken seriously the reviewer then tried to demonstrate the invalidity of the IQ measure at these lower grades. Is there, then, a demonstration that the total IQ, the measure for which the effects were significant only at the lower two grades, was poorly measured? No, indeed. We never see reference to total IQ again, apparently because it was too well-measured. Instead, we are given a detailed analysis of reasoning and verbal IQ, which together, make up total IQ. What the reader is not told by the reviewer is that *it is not true* that reasoning IQ, which is most criticized, showed expectancy effects at only the lower grades where it appeared to be less well-measured. As a matter of fact, 15 of 17 classrooms showed greater reasoning IQ gains among those randomly selected children who had been alleged to their teachers to be potential bloomers ($p = .001$). What if we drop those "poorly-measured" three first grade classrooms? Why, then it's 13 of 14

Reprinted from *American Educational Research Journal*, *6* (1969), 689-691, by permission of the American Educational Research Association.

classrooms that show the hypothesized outcome ($p = .001$). While we're tossing out "poorly-measured" classrooms, why not throw out the three second grade classrooms? That leaves us only 10 of 11 classes showing the hypothesized outcome ($p = .006$). It should be quite clear that the general results of the effects of teacher expectations on reasoning IQ do *not* depend upon the inclusion of the particular classrooms singled out by the reviewer.

In connection with his critique of the IQ scores reported, the reviewer made reference to a table that has as its upper and lower limits for total, verbal, and reasoning scores, mental age equivalents of 10.0 and 5.3. Such a table exists, it is true, but there is also a table, two pages earlier, that shows limits of MA from 16.5 to 0.5. In all cases IQ was defined, as might be expected, by the quite standard formula of MA/CA, and for the subtests, as well as for the full test, the full range of MAs was employed. Can we, now, explain a mean posttest IQ of 150 for the six children of the fast track classroom of the second grade who had been alleged to be potential bloomers? Indeed, we can! Their mean MA was simply 1.5 times the magnitude of their mean CA. The MAs were 16.5, 16.5, 10.0, 10.0, 10.0, and 8.9.

Now what can be said about the very low pretest reasoning IQs of the first grade children? Let us first be very clear that these low IQs reflect no clerical or scoring errors. These low IQs were earned because very few items were attempted by many of the children. The fact that *if* the children had attempted all items they would have earned a higher IQ is interesting but not invalidating. On any IQ test, not trying an item is likely to lower the score. If Flanagan (1960), in his development of TOGA, had intended the chance level of performance to be the basal MA level, he would not have tabulated the MA equivalent of a single item (out of 63) answered correctly!

The first grade children were not, of course, pretested by the first grade teachers. Careful reading of the *Pygmalion* book shows that the "first grade" children were pretested by their kindergarten teachers in the spring of the year. These kindergarten teachers were primarily responsible for assigning the children to the fast, medium, or slow track of the first grade on the basis of their kindergarten performance and without access to the IQ scores that Thorndike felt to be "worthless." We take the hypothesis of "worthlessness" seriously and submit it to empirical test. A worthless test cannot predict better than chance how a kindergarten teacher will subsequently assign pupils to the fast, medium, or slow tracks of a school. Yet children scoring higher on the "worthless" reasoning IQ pretest were far more likely to be assigned to faster tracks than were lower scoring children. The F with 2 and 60 df

was 24.05 (p < .001). When the track variable was split into a linear regression and deviation from regression component, F for linear regression (df 1, 60) was 45.88 (p < .001). Linear F and overall F were both associated with a correlation exceeding .65 (Friedman, 1968). For a "worthless" test, that's not too bad a validity coefficient. One can only wonder what tests the reviewer had in mind as examples of tests that were *really* valid!

There is even more dramatic evidence, however, to test the reviewer's hypothesis of "worthless" tests. If the tests are worthless, they ought not to predict what a different teacher will say about the child's likelihood of being successful in the future, one year after the child took the reasoning pretest, and without the teacher's having access to the IQ scores. Unhappily for the hypothesis of "worthlessness," the tests predict fairly well. The correlation between the reasoning IQ pretests taken at the end of the kindergarten year and a different teacher's prediction of the child's likelihood of being a future success, a prediction made one year later, was +.49 (N = 57, p < .001). Not a bad predictive validity for a "worthless" test.

The reviewer likened the invalidity of the reasoning IQ subtest to the faulty mechanism of a clock heard to chime more than 12 times. It should be pointed out that not every listener at Teachers College heard those extra chimes. Thus, in their review, Peter Gumpert (Teachers College) and Carol Gumpert (Albert Einstein College of Medicine) said: "The study provides a perfectly satisfactory demonstration that the teacher expectation effects hypothesized do indeed take place." (1968, p. 22) Readers, nevertheless, were advised by Thorndike to throw away the clock. But, in the words of an Asian colleague, "When a demonstrably adequate clock is cavalierly thrown away, we may question how sincerely the discarder wants to know what time it is."

References

Flanagan, John C., *Tests of General Ability: Technical Report.* Chicago; Science Research Associates, 1960.

Friedman, H., "Magnitude of Experimental Effect and a Table for its Rapid Estimation," *Psychological Bulletin* 70 (1968): 245-251.

Gumpert, P., and Gumpert, C., "The Teacher as Pygmalion: Comments on the Psychology of Expectation." *Urban Review 3*, 1 (1968): 21-25.

Rosenthal, Robert, and Jacobson, Lenore, *Pygmalion in the Classroom.* New York: Holt, Rinehart and Winston, 1968. 240 pp.

Thorndike, Robert L., Review of *Pygmalion in the Classroom. American Educational Research Journal 5,* (November 1968): 708-711.

But You Have to
Know How to Tell Time

Robert L. Thorndike

True enough, there *is* a table of age equivalents of raw scores that goes from 0.5 years to 16.5 years! (It is for the total score on TOGA.) But does one have to be so naive as to use it? On how many 6-month-old examinees was it based? And if no children were tested below about the age of 5 years, as seems likely, how secure is an extrapolation stretching downward 4 or 5 years?

Age equivalents represent about as unsatisfactory an approach to an equal-unit scale as we have, even during the elementary school years. When extrapolated far beyond the ages or grades in which testing was done, they become arbitrary, insecure, and largely meaningless.

Note that it is the *scale of measurement* that is being questioned, not the validity of the raw scores. The fact that a child did not understand what he was supposed to do, and consequently omitted all or most of the items, could be quite predictive of his academic status at the time or even a year later. However, it would still be nonsense to say that his mental age was 0.5 or 1.0 or 2.0. And it is the scale of measurement that becomes crucial for the authors' argument.

Incidentally, information on the number of omitted items seems quite central to any understanding of the effects of the experimental treatment. If there is one thing that extra encouragement by a teacher might readily do, whether given before or during an examination, it would be to lead a pupil to take a shot at two or three more items, whether he knew the answers or not. When score is simply the number of items right, as it is on TOGA and many other tests, normal luck could then produce a measurable if not a substantial increment in average score. At all ages, one would wish to see data on number attempted as well as number correct.

In closing, let me express a very real interest in the notion of the "self-fulfilling prophecy." I would expect the phenomenon to appear most clearly, to the extent that it is in fact effective, in those areas that are most directly teacher-based and school-dependent, such as learning to read, to write and to cipher. Perhaps others can

Reprinted from *American Educational Research Journal, 6* (1969): 692, by permission of the American Educational Research Association.

learn from *Pygmalion's* shortcomings, and carry out research on these problems that is psychometrically and experimentally adequate.

Review of
Pygmalion in the Classroom

Lewis R. Aiken, Jr.

The reader of this review will recognize Robert Rosenthal as the psychologist who, over the past few years, has been collecting evidence and stimulating research by others concerned with the effects of experimenter expectations on the results of experiments. Some of the evidence of such experiments, in which animals ranging from planaria to men have been employed as subjects, is reviewed in Chapter 4 of the present volume. In this book, however, the animals of primary interest are public school children and their teachers.

Rosenthal's general thesis is that ". . . one person's expectation for another person's behavior can quite unwittingly become a more accurate prediction simply for its having been made." After describing observational and experimental support for this hypothesis in clinic, laboratory, and everyday contexts, the authors proceed to detail a study conducted at a public elementary school in a lower class community; about one-sixth of the school population was Mexican. The purpose of the experiment was to determine what the effects would be of indicating to their teachers that a random sample of pupils will show a significant "spurt" in intellectual functioning, or "blooming," within a year or so. At the beginning of the academic year all of the children in the school were pretested with Flanagan's Test of General Ability to obtain total, verbal, and reasoning IQs. Twenty per cent of the children were identified as "potential spurters"—actually at random but ostensibly by means of the test—to their teachers. The same IQ test was readministered to all of the children in posttesting sessions one semester, one academic year, and two academic years later. Intellectual growth was defined as the difference between a child's pretest IQ and his IQ on one of the posttests. The major research questions was : Will the experimental group (expectancy group)

Reprinted from *Educational and Psychological Measurement, 29* (Spring 1969): 226-228, by permission. Mr. Aiken is associated with Guilford College.

show greater gains in IQ than a control group of the remaining children (all those not identified as "potential spurters")? In general, the expectancy children did show greater gains in IQ than the controls, although there were significant interactions between gain scores and grade level, nationality, sex, ability track, and other variables. For example, children in grades one and two, Mexican children, and those in the medium ability track showed the greatest initial gains; boys showed greater gains in verbal IQ and girls in reasoning IQ.

The gains shown by the expectancy group were not limited to IQ. They also gained more than controls in reading grades and were rated by their teachers as more intellectually curious, happier, and in less need of social approval than controls.

In spite of the rather dramatic changes shown by the expectancy children, the investigators were unable to identify any specific teacher behavior which might have caused such changes. The teachers did not appear to spend more time with the expectancy children and even failed to remember that many of them had been identified at the beginning of the year as "potential spurters." In his studies of experimenter effects, Rosenthal has confessed that he does not know precisely what experimenter behavior produces the effects, and the same admission can be made regarding the results of the present investigation. The authors speculate that the teacher treated the expectancy children differently from the controls— through facial expressions, postures, and perhaps touch, but they cite no evidence for this proposition.

Rosenthal and Gregory *(sic)*, like Fechner before them, have anticipated their critics by considering alternative explanations for the results, viz., test unreliability, pretest IQ differences, artifacts in the testing process, and other methodological flaws; they discuss and dismiss each of these in turn. And it may well be, as Fechner declared of his psychophysics, that the results of *Pygmalion in the Classroom* will stand because critics will not agree on how to explain them. Certainly Rosenthal and Gregory *(sic)* have produced a provocative experiment, and although critics should have no problem attacking it, the array of significant findings makes it difficult to destroy. It should be noted that the control group samples were much larger than the experimental groups, that gain scores are open to question, that many of the significant differences may have been caused by the scores of only a few children, and that the results of the present experiment are in direct contrast to those obtained by Judy Evans (p. 96). Nevertheless, even as a minimum accomplishment, the results once more call into question the meaning and stability of test scores and other evaluations. They also point to a need for a reassessment and more careful analysis of the effects of teacher behavior, both verbal and non-verbal, and teacher attitudes on the attitudes, self-concepts, and performance of school children.

What Can You Expect?

Robert Coles

The moment a child is born, it joins a particular kind of world. A doctor has done the delivery in a hospital, or a midwife has done it in a rural cabin, or the baby has emerged unassisted. That baby learns how to sit up, walk, talk, play, dress, and eat. Genes have a lot to do with the child's appearance and appetites and growth, but what happens to anyone, infant or grownup, is almost inevitably ordained by the laws of nature. A boy might have it in him to become a tall, strong, energetic man, and a girl might have it in her to become an unusual beauty, but without proper food they will not survive infancy, let alone reach adulthood in anything like the condition they might have attained, had life been more generous.

All this is common sense, but a common sense that is often missing in arguments over the rights and powers of those two antagonists "nature" and "nurture," each of which has its strenuous partisans. Nor is the struggle only abstract, ideological, or philosophical. When a subject such as what goes to make up "intelligence" is debated, very concrete and practical issues are involved. If intelligence is to be considered something fixed and precise, a biological "given," then teachers are right to separate the quick-witted child from the slow one, and to look upon themselves as agents for each kind of child: the child comes to school with a good, fast mind, an average one, or a slow one, and the school's job is to find out and act accordingly. This teacher works well with fast learners, that one with the dull child; So-and-So has a knack for those in the middle, who respond to her and go as far as they can as a result of her attentive ear, her light, gentle touch. On the other hand, "intelligence" can be considered a complicated and variable activity by which the mind, under certain circumstances—and what is favorable for one person can be the opposite for another—meets up with facts and situations and comes to understand them, act upon them, gain some control over them. This view places great stress on complexity and variability. Idiots can have as-

Reprinted from *The New Yorker*, © April 19, 1969, pp. 169-170. 173-177, by permission of the New Yorker Magazine, Inc.

tonishing powers of recall; geniuses can be dumb about so very much; writers can barely know how to count; any number of brilliant social scientists can't write a straight sentence. More to the point of our present national problems, children can be stubbornly, impossibly backward in school but shrewd, imaginative, and resourceful at home—or, more likely, on the streets and in the alleys.

At this point, the anthropologist and the psychiatrist (and perhaps the merely intelligent teacher or parent) may remind us that some children grow up in a family, a neighborhood, a town where schools mean a lot and the children's achievement in them means everything to their parents. Such children learn that it makes a difference if they pay attention to the teacher and do what she says; others literally learn not to learn. One boy's parents are well-to-do and ambitious, but he is afraid to learn and so has what child psychiatrists call a "learning block." His brain seems normal but his mind won't, for any number of reasons, take in the facts and put them together. A blurred, indistinct world seems safer—an attitude obviously the result of certain experiences. Many children have no such psychological problem but still don't do well at school—because they come there, as it is now put, "disadvantaged" and "deprived." A number of physicians and nutritionists and neurophysiologists argue that a diet low in critically important vitamins, minerals, and proteins causes serious damage to an infant's brain, so he comes to school retarded not by disease or injury but by the repercussions of a nation's social and economic problem, which becomes an intense personal problem for millions of families. Yet even if poor parents can provide their children with decent meals and medical care and clothes—which is not usual—there is a larger issue. Do parents give their children confidence, or do they feel discouraged about life most of the time? It takes a lot of persuasion, subtle suggestion, charm, or even force to make an infant the kind of child teachers like: well scrubbed, eager, obedient, responsive. Mothers who live in broken-down tenements, who never know when the next few dollars will come, have little energy left for their children. Life is grim and hard, and the child has to learn that. He learns it and learns it and learns it— how to survive all sorts of threats and dangers, why his parents have given up on school, why they have fallen on their faces. He learns about racial hatred, the state of the economy, technological change; he learns whether he is an insider or an outsider, whether storekeepers and property owners and policemen treat his family with kindness and respect or with suspicion and even out-and-out contempt. By the time a child of the ghetto comes to school, his knowledge might well be what has been awkwardly called "the intelligence of the so-called unintelligent as it appears in sly, devious, and haunting ways."

The teacher may know all that but have little time to ponder the social and psychological forces that make children so very different from one another before they have had a single day of school. To the teacher, the differences are a beginning, not an end. Six-year-old children are what they are, and they are quickly found out by their teachers and school psychologists and by "objective criteria" —by all those intelligence tests, each with its own twist, its own special, prideful, reasonable (or extravagant) claims. These tests are employed to separate children by "tracks": fast, medium, slow. The theory is valid; the able and gifted ones will not intimidate the fearful and slow ones, nor will the slow ones cost the fast ones their right to learn at a speed they find congenial. Yet those who score well in the tests take an interest in schoolwork and become known as first-rate students; those to whom teachers and the work they assign are a big bore or a big fright become the "problem child," the "disruptive child," the slow-witted or stupid one—no matter how bright they may be "underneath."

Well, what can the poor overworked, underpaid teacher do about all that? Can he be responsible for our nation's injustices, for its history of racial strife, for the regional circumstances that doom white Appalachian children and Indian children and Mexican-American children as well as black children? Can schools make up for lacks and shortages and cruelties at home? Can a few hours in a classroom, even one run by the most capable and best-intentioned of teachers, really change a sullen, troubled child's destiny? Can it be that teachers in dozens of ways, for dozens of reasons, determine which children will eagerly absorb their lessons and which ones will say maybe or positively no? Can the child's performance in school be considered the result as much of what his teachers' attitudes are toward him as of his native intelligence or his attitude as a pupil?

A book with the dramatic and suggestive title of *Pygmalion in the Classroom* (Holt, Rinehart and Winston) has a lot to say about the whole issue. The authors are Robert Rosenthal, a Harvard social psychologist, and Lenore Jacobson, a San Francisco school principal, and their study has to do, in the pedantic words of their subtitle, with "teacher expectation and pupils' intellectual development." They began their work in 1964, when they gave the "Harvard Test of Inflected Acquisition" to most of the children of what they have called the Oak School, an elementary establishment on the West Coast. (The only ones not tested were to leave the school before the next round of tests.) The test had prophetic powers, the school's teachers were told: "As a part of our study we are further validating a test which predicts the likelihood that a child will show an inflection point or 'spurt' within the near future. This test which will be administered in your school will allow us to predict which youngsters are most likely to show an academic spurt. The top twenty per cent (approximately) of the scorers on this test will probably be found at various levels of academic functioning. The development of the test for predicting inflections or 'spurts' is not yet such that every one of the top twenty per cent of the children will show a more significant inflection or spurt in their learning within the next year or less than will the remaining eighty per cent of the children."

There is no "Harvard Test of Inflected Acquisition." Dr. Rosenthal and Mrs. Jacobson had a mission to fulfill, and they knew that such a name would impress schoolteachers of the second half of the twentieth century; when someone out of Harvard comes around to estimate "inflected acquisition," a woman who struggles to teach boys and girls their letters and numbers can only be grateful for the assistance afforded by Progress and Science. The children were really given the useful Flanagan's Tests of General Ability, or TOGA. TOGA is one of a hundred tests most teachers don't know about. They do know, however, that social scientists are smart. So the Oak School teachers had reason to believe they were aiding research by lending their children to an experiment that would help establish the value of yet another manmade "instrument"—the name given all those questionnaires and tests by the psychologists and sociologists who make them up. Naturally, the teachers also believed that they would become privy to interesting and important information. The Oak School divides each grade into fast, medium, and slow tracks, and TOGA supposedly supplied lists of pupils for all three tracks of each grade. TOGA apparently could spot the "spurters," or "bloomers," and the teachers were let in on the discoveries, though they were cautioned not to tell what they knew to any children or parents. But what really happened was that Dr. Rosenthal and Mrs. Jacobson had arbitrarily selected the names; the TOGA scores had nothing to do with it. A third-grade class made up of fast learners might supply only one or two children to the honor roll of the "Harvard Test of Inflected Acquisition," and a first-grade class that seemed extremely slow might present eight or nine children headed for better things indeed. If any of the children on the lists turned out to be "special," it was because their teachers were told they were or were going to be.

Teachers have a lot to do besides reading and rereading the names of a few children who just might be headed for a kind nod from fate, and the Oak School went about its regular business for a year, interrupted only by two more bouts with TOGA. Then our two authors returned to Cambridge with the "data." Teachers are always grading their pupils—how they are getting along in each subject, how they behave, what their "attitude" is. All that, too, went East to the computers. The teachers were asked for more information: How successful might the children be; were their achievements in class the result of native ability or, say, a capacity for pure drudgery; was this child "appealing, well adjusted, affectionate" and that one "hostile and motivated by a need for approval"? What did the authors and their research assistants discover? Their report—*Pygmalion in the Classroom*—is full of charts and graphs and statistics and precentages and carefully weighed statements, but there are conclusions that have great significance for this nation, preoccupied as it is with severe educational problems of many kinds. Among the children of the first and second grades, those tagged "bloomers" made astonishing gains in the later tests: "About every fifth control-group child gained twenty IQ points or more, but of the special children, nearly every second child gained that much."

The lesson in the book is clear: All sorts of young children did very much better in school than others like them, presumably because their teachers *expected* them to become "bloomers, and TOGA's putative prophecy was fulfilled so conclusively that even hardline social scientists were startled. They were also taken aback by other results. The greatest gains were among the Mexican-American children, a "minority group" with "cultural disadvantage" and "cultural deprivation." Despite these condescending labels, the Mexican children became much better students in their teachers' eyes, too. What is more, the children who looked classically Mexican did better than those who looked a little "Anglo," which prompts the authors to speculate, dryly, that "the teachers' pre-experimental expectancies of the more Mexican-looking boys' intellectual performance was probably lowest of all. These children may have had the most to gain by the introduction of a more favorable expectation into the minds of their teachers." But the teachers were not won over by the remarkable improvement; the Mexican children still were rated low in "adjustment" and intellectual curiosity. Harvard people might know something, the teachers appeared to agree, but these miraculous improvements had come about because of something that had nothing to do with the teachers and their attitudes as educators, as men and women who believe in some children and view others, right from the start, as hopeless. Yet maybe a teacher can silently let a child know that good things are, incredibly, around the corner because the experts say so. A teacher's faith is apparently not required—only her loyalty to experts, the secular gods of the twentieth century. Dr. Rosenthal and Mrs. Jacobson are quite aware of the effect a pair of scientists armed with tons of paper can have on opinions. What obviously surprised them was the substantial and persisting nature of that effect, obtained in spite of the long-standing prejudices of teachers. "One wonders whether among these minority-group children who over-represent the slow track and the disadvantaged of Oak School their gains in intellectual competence may not be easier for teachers to bring about than to believe."

The prejudices of teachers—and the effects the prejudices have on learning—come across on almost every page of this book. Bright children who were labelled "bloomers" were found more pleasant and attractive by their teachers; slow children labelled "bloomers" were grudgingly viewed as "more autonomous but less affectionate." When children in the lowest track inexplicably improved, the teachers became confused and angry: "The more such a child gained in IQ, the more unfavorably he was evaluated by his teacher in almost every respect." The authors remark, ironically, that "if a child is to show intellectual gains, it may be better for his intellectual vitality and for his mental health as seen by his teacher, if his teacher has been expecting him to gain intellectually. It appears that there may be psychological hazards to unexpected intellectual growth."

What actually happened in the Oak School? The authors of *Pygmalion in the Classroom* admit that they don't know. Before they tell about their project, they offer a more general discussion of what I suppose is best called the "self-fulfilling prophecy" as it takes place in everyday life, in the practice of medicine and psychiatry, and in the education not only of children but even of animals. Banks have failed simply because frightened people believed them to be in trouble. Certain groups of people have always been considered to be by nature inferior and uneducable, and because they have been treated so, they have appeared so, behaved so, and confirmed the beliefs of their oppressors. And patients feel better, get better, because they are persuaded that a given pill will do its job. There is evidence that even something as tangible as surgery draws upon psychological overtones for its success. In 1961, Henry K. Beecher, professor of anesthesiology at the Harvard Medical School, published in the *Journal of the American Medical Association* an article called "Surgery as Placebo." He described a new operation to relieve angina pectoris, and reported that the benefits of it were the result "of what happened in the minds of the patients and the surgeons involved." Experiments revealed that surgeons who believed enthusiastically in the new method brought relief to patients four times as often as the skeptical surgeons did. It even turned out that a feigned operation, done under anesthesia and believed by the patient to be a complicated surgery, was equally effective. Psychiatry has not even begun to settle the issue of which treatment works for what reason. Entire mental hospitals have been suddenly transformed by the arrival of a new drug or "technique," and just as quickly the old despair and gloom have reap-

peared. Psychiatric theorists argue fiercely, attack one another in
dense, muddled language—often enough to conceal from themselves, let alone others, the ever-present hunch that the mind is
healed not only by rational explanations, however intricate and
compelling, but by experiences (in the doctor's office, outside his
office) that have to do with faith, reassurance, suggestion, persuasion, all of which a doctor can first inspire or offer out of his
heart, and later nervously dress up in elaborate language that is re-
spectably scientific.

"To summarize now what has been learned from research
employing animal subjects generally," the authors say, "it seems
that those that are expected to perform competently tend to do so,
while animals expected to perform incompetently tend also to perform as prophesied." In describing an experiment, Dr. Rosenthal
relates animals to children in a way every teacher might think
about: "At the beginning of that study experimenters assigned
allegedly dull animals were of course told that they would find retarded learning on the part of their rats. They were, however, reas-
sured that 'it has been found that even the dullest rats can, in time,
learn the required responses.' Animals alleged to be dull, then,
were described as educable but slow. It was interesting in the light
of this to learn that of the experimenters who had been assigned
'dull' animals, forty-seven per cent believed their subjects to be
uneducable. Only five per cent of the experimenters assigned
'bright' rats were equally pessimistic about their animal's future.
From this result one wonders about the beliefs created in schoolteachers when they are told a child is educable but slow, deserving
but disadvantaged."

In the Oak School, "disadvantaged" children suddenly came to
life and made astonishing gains. Yet they were given no crash programs, no special tutoring, no trips to museums; their teachers
were simply told that those particular children bore watching.
Another research project is needed if we are to discover how teachers go about letting children know they have a special destiny. No
doubt dozens of signals are made: gestures, postures, facial expressions, a manner of approach, a choice of words and the way they
are spoken, a look in the eyes, a touch of the hand. Soon the child
gets the message—perhaps in the best way, unself-consciously. He
begins to feel the teacher's feelings, the pleasure of approval, and
begins to learn more. There comes a time when the issue is not
only emotional but intellectual, when a teacher's expectations
become a child's sense of prideful achievement, which in turn en-
ables him to expect more—of himself.

Pygmalion in the Classroom is not meant to be a popular book,
though as books written by social scientists go it possesses an ex-
ceptionally accessible narrative style. The writers are not afraid of

a readable and lively sentence, and they mix blunt social comment with the most complicated statistical equations and tabulations. Without attempting eloquence, they have achieved the matter-of-fact eloquence that goes with an original, imaginative study of people and their doings with one another. The authors constantly remind us of the ethical dimensions of scientific work. After all, they might have persuaded the teachers of Oak School to think less of certain children and to feel right about expecting nothing—right because scientists have said that it is useless to expect much but decline in certain children.

I like the way Dr. Rosenthal and Mrs. Jacobson question themselves, their moral purposes, and state their loyalties—utlimately to man as more than the sum of all labels and categories, and to man as full of hidden as well as apparent possibilities, for the good and for the bad. And I also like the title of this book. At the end, Eliza Doolittle is quoted: "The difference between a lady and a flower girl is not how she behaves, but how she's treated." In Shaw's *Pygmalion* a professor helps make a slattern into a lady, but in the Greek legend the issue is more momentous, a matter of life and death—which is what the alternatives are for our schoolchildren.

Great Expectations

Herbert Kohl

Most educational research focuses upon the success and failure of students or on the economic "effectiveness" of school systems. But there seems to be a tacit agreement between teachers and researchers (usually psychologists and sociologists) not to raise questions concerning the teachers themselves. It is difficult for researchers to enter a school to study teacher behavior, and they rarely do so. Yet two researchers, Robert Rosenthal, a psychologist, and Lenore Jacobson, a school administrator, have violated the non-aggression pact between teachers and researchers and studied the manipulation of teacher behavior in the classroom. *Pygmalion in the Classroom* is a report on the effect of a teacher's expectations upon the performance of his pupils. The study is ingenious and the results obtained highly significant.

Rosenthal and Jacobson are concerned with self-fulfilling

prophecies—i.e., those predictions of future events that become central factors in bringing about predicted events.* As they say, "the central proposition of this book is that one person's prophecy of another's intellectual performance can come to determine that other's intellectual performance." They got the faculty of a school in South San Francisco to cooperate with them by pretending that they were conducting a scientific study of the performance of certain students in the school who were "late bloomers." An official document describing the project was presented to the teachers:

STUDY OF REFLECTED ACQUISITION
(Harvard-National Science
Foundation)

All children show hills, plateaus, and valleys in their scholastic progress. The study being conducted at Harvard with the support of the National Science Foundation is interested in those children who show an unusual forward spurt of academic and intellectual functioning. When these spurts occur in children who have not been functioning too well academically, the result is familiarly referred to as "late blooming."

As a part of our study we are further validating a test which predicts the likelihood that a child will show an inflection point or "spurt" within the near future. This test which will be administered in your school will allow us to predict which youngsters are most likely to show an academic spurt. The top 20 percent (approximately) of the scorers on this test will probably be found at various levels of academic functioning.

The development of the test for predicting inflections or "spurts" is not yet such that *every* one of the top 20 percent will show the spurt or "blooming" effect. But the top 20 percent of the children *will* show a more significant inflection or spurt in their learning within the next year or less than will the remaining 80 percent of the children.

Because of the experimental nature of the tests, basic principles of test construction do not permit us to discuss the test or test scores either with the parents or the children themselves.

Upon completion of this study, participating districts will be advised of the results.

There is no "inflected acquisition," of course, nor is there a "test of late blooming." Students were given an ordinary test of intelligence and achievement, but one unfamiliar to the teachers; "late bloomers" were selected at random from the student body. The teachers were then told that some of their pupils had turned

---

[1]An example of a self-fulfilling prophecy is a favorable medical prognosis in a case of a cancer which caused the patient to move from despair to hope and became a crucial part of his cure.

The implications of the study described in *Pygmalion in the Classroom* also extend beyond education. For Rosenthal and Jacobson's research methods also involved the manipulation of teachers, whose cooperation was enlisted in bad faith. The researchers assumed god-like roles; they were the only people in the school who knew what the "experiment" was all about and who were not themselves the subjects. They presumed their involvement was neutral and that their work was simply an attempt to uncover "objective" (though statistical) knowledge. Yet can a social science "experiment" involving the manipulation of human beings be neutral? Moreover, what is the moral and human cost of acquiring knowledge through deceit and bad faith? This study does not reveal what the teachers who have been studied feel, nor whether they have learned something about themselves that could have some effect.

The results of Rosenthal's work are, of course, gratifying. They confirm what many critics of the schools have been saying. Yet an approach which is itself so totalitarian makes one question the value of acquiring knowledge by treating people as objects of an experiment. Surely there must be a more direct way of confronting teachers with their attitudes, and studying them in a more direct way. We do not need more people in the schools who cannot be trusted, even if they happen to be social scientists.

Appendix A:
Details of the Reanalysis

In this section we discuss in detail the methodological problems involved in the analysis of such a complex study, comment on RJ's choice of analysis, and present the results of our reanalyses.

RJ applied a standard analytic procedure, analysis of variance, without discussion of its assumptions or applicability and little attempt at exploration of the many other possibilities for analysis. Is an analysis of variance approach the most appropriate for this experiment? What about investigating the relationships between pre- and posttest scores via regression analysis? What about analysis by classroom? What about nonparametric analyses?

Given the choice of a standard analysis of variance, we can ask whether the five particular factors—treatment, grade, track, sex, minority group status—should be included in the design. Can the number of cells be reduced in other ways than by dropping factors completely? Why choose simple gain scores as the criterion variable? Do the gain scores used satisfy the assumptions necessary for a standard analysis of variance to give valid results? Why not use posttest scores alone? Covariance analysis? A repeated measures analysis? Is unweighted means analysis the appropriate way to calculate these analyses of variance: What about unweighted least squares? Weighted least squares? While the main issue is whether analysis of variance is appropriate at all, we include discussions of the other questions.

These many analyses are included to show the inconsistency of results from one method to another and are not necessarily valid analyses. The problems of unbalanced sampling plan, 20% subject loss, many extreme scores, and low reliability cast doubt on the validity of the statistical procedures reported. That is, one can never be sure in a given analysis how close the nominal p-value is to the actual probability of rejecting the null hypothesis when it is true. In fact, it is not clear that any analysis or significance test on these data can be accepted as wholly valid. It is only by examining the data from many different aspects that we are finally able to make any over-all "conclusions."

Extreme Scores

In Chapter IV we noted the existence of many extreme scores in the RJ data. Very low scores are an indication that children responded randomly, consistently incorrectly, or did not respond at all to many questions; very high scores indicate that near the upper limits of the test the norming process is inadequate. Neither score gives an indication of the child's "true" mental ability. When there are so many extreme scores, it is difficult to know how to analyze the data. Even if we were to regard these scores as valid, their presence creates score distributions which are nonnormal, skewed, and likely to have different variances in different subgroups. Applying standard statistical procedures to such scores may create a serious difference between the true and nominal significance levels of any statistical procedure (R. M. Elashoff, 1968). (See the section on reliability in Chapter IV for an example of this.)

What procedures might be used to avoid such problems? Of course, the best way is to choose a measuring instrument and to plan data collection so that such scores do not arise. Perhaps the next best approach with the RJ data is to analyze the raw scores. This removes the problem of inadequate norming but forces us to analyze scores from the three different TOGA forms separately. As we shall see in later sections this is really necessary even using IQ scores. We have included analyses of total raw scores for first and second graders.

However, if analysis of the data in IQ form is still desired some procedure must be used to handle scores outside the main norming range of 60–160. One procedure is to *truncate* the data by excluding as too poorly measured any IQ scores outside this range. Another possibility is *renorming* the data by replacing all scores less than 60 by 60 and all scores higher than 160 by 160. Neither procedure is wholly adequate since the effect on various statistical approaches is unknown, but analyzing the data in all three ways, in original IQ form, in truncated IQ form, and in renormed IQ form provides information on the sensitivity of the results to the presence of extreme scores. Other possible procedures are trimming or winsorization, where a certain percentage of top and bottom scores are excluded or altered (see Dixon and Massey,

1969), or use of a statistical model accounting for the presence of outliers (J. D. Elashoff, 1970).

Table 8 shows the effects of these three procedures on the test-retest correlation of total scores for first and second graders. Note that the values are highest using raw scores. Other differences in the effects of these options will appear in sections to follow.

TABLE 8

Test-retest Correlations for

First and Second Grades Total IQ

		Control	Experimental
Raw Scores		.73	.87
IQ Scores --	All	.66	.72
	Renormed	.68	.75
	Truncated	.70	.67

Relationships Between Pre and Post Scores

The basic aim of the RJ experiment was to assess the relationship between pretest and posttest scores in the experimental and control groups, to locate any significant differences between the groups, and to assess the importance of these differences. The first thing to do then is to examine the relationship between pretest and posttest in detail.

Regression Analyses

Scatterplots in Figures 11-19 show posttest IQ plotted against pretest IQ for Total, Verbal, and Reasoning scores for experimental and control groups of first and second graders, third and fourth graders, and fifth and sixth graders. This breakdown corresponds to the three different TOGA forms; further breakdown produces sample sizes too small for reasonable regression analyses. Experimental children are designated by X's, control children by dots. Norm limits are shown by the box drawn at 60 and 160 for both tests. The regression lines using all data and truncated data (all points outside the box deleted) are shown for both experi-

TABLE 9

Slope of Regression Line for Sex by Treatment by Grade Group[*]
Pretest to Basic Posttest

Total IQ

	Control		Experimental	
Grades	Female	Male	Female	Male
1 and 2	.62	.51	.72	1.03
3 and 4	.89	.92	1.12	.92
5 and 6	1.05	.94	1.14	1.07

[*]These twelve slopes are significantly nonparallel

$F_{11,296} = 2.59$ (p<.05)

TABLE 10

Slope of Regression Line for Treatment by Grade Group
Pretest to Basic Posttest

	Total IQ		Verbal IQ		Reasoning IQ	
	C	E	C	E	C	E
Grades 1 and 2						
IQ Scores	.56	.93	.72	.95	.32	.60
Renormed IQ	.62	.71	.63	.75	.58	.62
Truncated IQ	.69	.58	.66	.62	.61	.45
Raw Scores	.54	.45				
Grades 3 and 4						
IQ Scores	.90	.99	1.03	1.07	.88	.88
Renormed IQ	.89	.95	.91	.75	.71	.88
Truncated IQ	.84	.96	.87	.64	.53	.88
Grades 5 and 6						
IQ Scores	1.01	1.13	1.03	1.14	.82	.90
Renormed IQ	1.01	1.13	.90	.97	.81	.87
Truncated IQ	1.00	1.09	.87	.89	.76	.77

mental and control children. Note that the lines labelled T are for *truncated* data. Points off the graphs are indicated by arrows. Figure 20 provides the scatterplot and regression analysis for total raw scores for first and second graders.

Looking at the plots for first and second graders, one notices in Figure 11, for example, how strongly the one child with a posttest Total IQ of 202 affects the position of the regression line for the experimental group. The slope decreases from .93 to .58 when that one child is removed. The regression lines for experimental and control groups are generally closer together for the truncated data. Note that nearly 40% of the Reasoning IQ scores in Figure 13 appear well outside the norming ranges, most of them less than 60; 8 pretest scores are zero.

Is the relationship between pretest and postest the same across treatments, grades, sexes? Are the relationships linear? Are the slopes near unity? How much do extreme scores affect the relationships? Tables 9 and 10 show regression slopes calculated using the original IQ data, renormed IQ scores, truncated IQ scores for each grade group, each treatment group, and Total, Verbal, and Reasoning IQs, as well as for some raw score data.

First, let us examine regression slopes for Total IQ in twelve groups—grade x sex x treatment, see Table 9. These twelve regression lines are significantly nonparallel, but within the six treatments by grade groups, there are no significant slope differences between the sexes. (Questions could be raised about the validity of the F tests for parallelism in view of the extreme scores; however, slopes for males and females seem generally close enough to warrant combining the sexes to obtain larger sample sizes.)

Accordingly, males and females were combined in subsequent analyses. With the sexes combined, we compared slopes for treatment and control groups. There was a significant difference in slopes only for the first and second grades (this difference is almost solely due to the one boy with a posttest IQ of 202), although the slope for the experimental group was slightly higher in all three grade groups. The major differences in slopes appear to be between grade levels, the slopes in the first two grades being considerably lower than those for the higher grades which are near 1.0. The same basic conclusions hold for Verbal and Reasoning IQ scores, although for Reasoning IQ the slopes are somewhat less than 1.0 even for the upper grades.

What effects do the extreme scores have on the regression slopes? Renorming and truncation procedures generally reduce the slopes and remove their apparent tendency to be higher in the experimental group. Except for the third and fourth grades, these procedures have reduced differences in slope between the experimental and control groups. Except for the first and second grade experimental group, different procedures produced very similar slopes for the reasonably reliable Total IQ but produced strikingly different slopes for Verbal and Reasoning IQ, which contained scores far outside the norming ranges. Examination of the scatterplots produces some doubt about assuming a linear relationship between pre and post scores for Verbal and Reasoning IQ.

Choice of Criterion Measure

To determine whether posttest scores for the experimental group are higher than for the control group, we must choose a grouping of the data (by classroom, by grade, etc.) and a criterion variable. We have a pretest measure T_1 and a posttest measure T_3. (The time 2 and time 4 IQ scores can be treated similarly. We ignore the repeated measures aspect of the data for the moment.) The three basic approaches are to examine T_3 (or posttest) alone, to use $T_3 - T_1$ (or simple gain), or to use T_3 with T_1 as a covariate. Each of these choices rests on an implicit set of assumptions about the data. If the particular assumptions necessary for an approach are not satisfied the results obtained by applying the approach may not be valid. We must examine the data to determine which approach is most appropriate.

RJ rely solely on simple gain scores $T_3 - T_1$ arguing that ". . . postest only measures are less precise than the change or gain scores. . . ." (p. 108)† As we shall see, this oversimplified claim is actually false for the Reasoning IQ scores (Table 19).

Using posttest only (T_3) as a criterion requires the fewest assumptions. Assignment to treatment must be random and score distributions should be approximately normal with similar variances in both groups. We note that where the sample sizes of the two groups are quite different, as in the RJ study, this assumption of equal variances is much more important. Potentially, analysis of variance of T_3 only is the procedure most seriously affected by initial differences between groups. For comparison with other methods assume that the within-group variance using posttest scores is σ_ϵ^2.

If the within-group correlation between pre and posttest scores, ρ, is high, gain scores and covariance analysis can be expected to be more precise than analysis of variance of posttest scores. Using either gains or covariance requires random assignment to treatments and a similar relationship between pre and post scores in both groups. To derive formulas for the precision of gain scores or covariance analysis, we must adopt a model for the relationship between pre and posttest scores. We follow the general formulation of W.G. Cochran (1968) and assume that in the absence of

FIGURE 11: TOTAL IQ GRADES 1 & 2

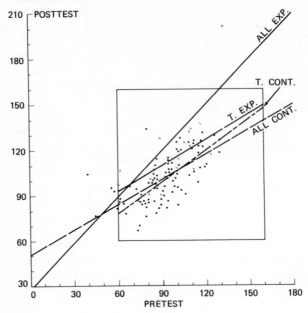

FIGURE 12: VERBAL IQ GRADES 1 & 2

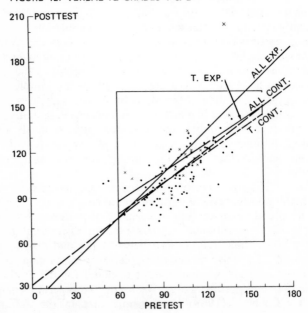

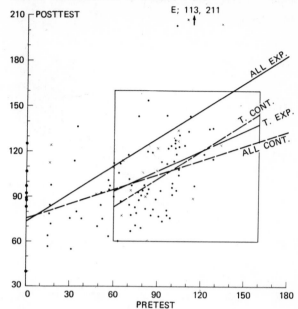

FIGURE 13: REASONING IQ GRADES 1 & 2

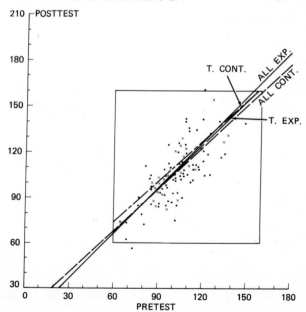

FIGURE 14: TOTAL IQ GRADES 3 & 4

FIGURE 15: VERBAL IQ GRADES 3 & 4

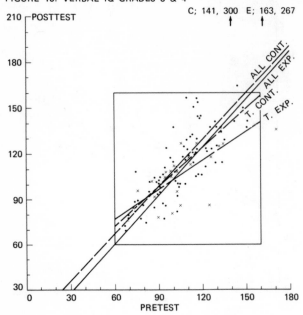

FIGURE 16: REASONING IQ GRADES 3 & 4

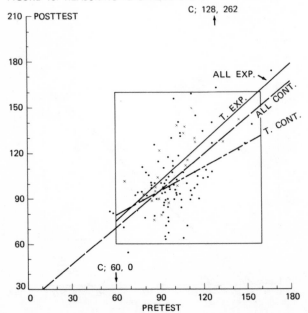

FIGURE 17: TOTAL IQ GRADES 5 & 6

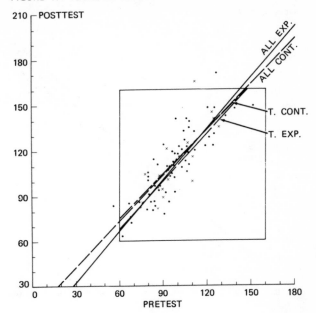

FIGURE 18: VERBAL IQ GRADES 5 & 6

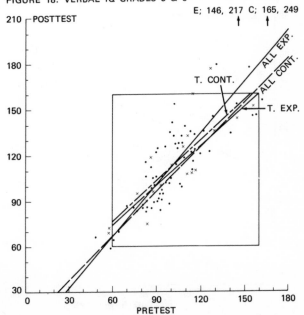

FIGURE 19: REASONING IQ GRADES 5 & 6

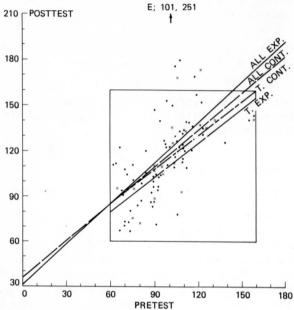

FIGURE 20: TOTAL RAW SCORE FIRST AND SECOND GRADES

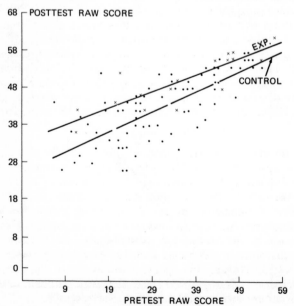

measurement errors, y or posttest has a linear regression on x (pretest)

$$y = \alpha + \beta x + \epsilon .$$

The observed scores, X and Y however, do contain measurement error $Y = y + u$ and $X = x + v$, and we can write:

$$Y = \alpha' + \beta'X + \epsilon' .$$

Under certain general conditions of independence and normality of variables, we find that the residual within-group error variance in covariance analysis will be about

$$\sigma^2_{\epsilon'} = \sigma^2_{\epsilon} (1 - \rho^2 R_X R_Y)$$

where ρ is the correlation between y and x and R_X and R_Y are the reliabilities $(R_X = \frac{\sigma^2_x}{\sigma^2_x + \sigma^2_v})$. (Note that the correlation between observed scores X and Y is $\rho\sqrt{R_X R_Y}$.)

Use of covariance analysis rests on a number of important assumptions about the underlying structure of the data (see Appendix B and J. D. Elashoff, 1969). In the absence of measurement error ($R_X = R_Y = 1$), then, covariance analysis can be expected to reduce the error variance by about $100\rho^2\%$; thus ρ must be larger than .3 for covariance analysis to reduce the error variance appreciably. The less reliable the pretest and posttest the greater ρ must be before covariance will be much more precise than analysis of variance on posttest scores alone; in addition, when the pretest is measured with error, covariance procedures generally underestimate the slope and undercorrect for pretest differences.

The use of gain scores makes the implicit assumption that $\beta' = 1.0$, i.e., that the regression of observed posttest on observed pretest has a regression slope of unity. If this is the case, analysis of variance of gain scores will give nearly the same results as analysis of covariance. If not, the error variance can be expected to be about

$$\sigma^2_g = \sigma^2_{\epsilon} \{ \frac{(2\beta'-1)}{\beta'^2} (1-\rho^2 R_Y R_X) + \frac{(\beta'-1)^2}{\beta'^2} \}$$

which is always greater than $\sigma^2_{\epsilon'}$ for $\beta' \neq 1$. Note that these variance figures are derived for large samples; for smaller samples imprecision due to the estimation of β will make $\sigma^2_{\epsilon'}$ larger. Little is known about the comparative robustness of these two procedures. Comparisons of two groups using gain scores will be misleading when the regression slope of post on pre is not unity for both groups or the pretest score distributions are different in the two groups; since in either case their use would not properly adjust for pretest differences. In a general discussion of this topic, L.J. Cronbach and L. Furby (1970) have suggested that gain scores are rarely useful for any purpose in educational research.

Using these formulas, we can predict whether posttest scores or gain scores will have smaller error variance for the RJ experiment by referring to evidence contained in RJ's Table A-30. We find a pretest-posttest correlation for the total school of approximately .75 for Total IQ and Verbal IQ but only about .50 for Reasoning IQ. Thus assuming that $_{\beta'} = 1$, using gain scores should provide a decrease in error variance of about 50% for Total IQ and Verbal IQ and none at all for Reasoning IQ. Referring to Table 19 in the analysis of variance section, we find that for two types of analysis of variance actually performed the decrease in error variance obtained by using gain scores was about 33% for Total IQ and 50% for Verbal IQ but that error variance *increased* by about 8% for Reasoning IQ. So, for Reasoning IQ, a posttest criterion is *not* less precise than a gain criterion. (Differences between the predicted and observed decreases in error variance occur because the formulas are for large samples, and because the correlations taken from Table A-30 were computed with all groups combined while the correlation in the formula is the within-group correlation.)

Thus, careful examination of these score distributions, scatterplots, and regression slopes suggests which scores are reasonable to analyze, whether grades (or TOGA forms) can be combined, and which analytic procedures seem appropriate.

If IQ scores are to be used, all analyses should be based on Total IQ; Verbal and Reasoning subscores are unreliable and inadequately normed in all grades. The only over-all analysis combining all grade groups that seems reasonably justified is analysis of posttest Total IQ scores. If random assignment to treatments can be assumed, analysis of posttest Total IQ scores is unbiased. In view of the lack of assurance on this question, however, and the higher pretest scores shown by the experimental group (see Tables 20-22), the results of such an analysis must also be interpreted with caution. Covariance analysis or gain score analysis using all grades is unwise because of the dissimilarity in pre-posttest relationships across grades. Using raw scores, the three forms of TOGA are not comparable.

Grades 3 and 4 and Grades 5 and 6 might reasonably be combined and analysis of Total IQ here, using covariance analysis (or analysis of variance of gains), would not be unreasonable. There seems little reason to perform separate analyses for males and females. Grades 1 and 2 present a more difficult problem, however. Here, gain scores are especially suspect because the pre-to-posttest slope is substantially less than one and the groups differ on the pretest. Covariance analysis should not be used with all IQ scores included because of the difference in slopes between groups, though it might be useful for renormed or truncated scores. Both posttest only and covariance analysis may be inadequate because of the large group differences in the pretest, as well as its unreliability. Analysis using raw scores seems most desirable. This could eliminate some of the problems caused by inadequate norming of the test. For first and second graders, test-retest correlations are higher for raw data and the regression slopes between pre-and posttest are similar for experimental and control groups.

Investigation
of Treatment Effects
Using Stepwise Regression

It is most important to assess the magnitude of any "significant" treatment effects observed. One approach to this problem is stepwise regression, see Appendix B. Taking posttest IQ as the dependent variable, we can determine how much of the variance in posttest scores is accounted for by linear regression on pretest IQ scores, treatment, sex, and other interesting variables.

First, we performed separate analyses for each of the three grade groups using the third or "basic" Total IQ score as criterion. Pretest Total IQ, treatment group, track, sex and minority-group status were included as predictor variables. In the analysis, pretest Total IQ was forced into the equation first and treatment was second; the other variables were left free to enter in any order. Results are shown in Table 11. These analyses must be interpreted with caution because of the extreme scores in Total IQ for grades 1 and 2 and because the other variables are categorical. In addition, for a dichotomous variable such as treatment, R^2 is lower when the number in each group is not the same than when the split is 50-50; R^2 for a 20-80 split will be roughly 2/3 of R^2 for a 50-50 split given the same difference in Total IQ means. Moreover, the predictor variables are not independent and their contributions overlap. Thus these analyses must be regarded as giving at most a rough approximation of the relative importance of the predictor variables. Pretest Total IQ predicts 43%, 63%, and 72% of the variance in posttest Total IQ for grades 1-2, grades 3-4, grades 5-6, respectively. Including all the variables accounts for a total of 55%, 70%, and 75% respectively of the variance in posttest. For grades 3-4 and 5-6, treatment accounted for less than 1% of the variance in posttest Total IQ scores; treatment accounted for 7% of the variance in grades 1-2. No attempt has been made to assess the statistical significance of these increases in R^2 because of the difficulties mentioned earlier. Our only purpose is to gain an impression of the relative importance of any treatment effect.

As we remarked earlier, total raw scores seemed a more desirable criterion measure than Total IQ for grades 1 and 2. The

TABLE 11

Results of Stepwise Regression Analyses for

Grade Groups 1 and 2, 3 and 4, 5 and 6

Criterion Variable: Total IQ on Basic Posttest

Predictors: Total IQ Pretest, Treatment, Track, Sex,
Minority-Group Status

Criterion	Step	Variable Entered	F to Enter	R^2	Increase in R^2
Grades 1 & 2	1 forced	Total IQ 1	85	.43	.43
Total IQ 3	2 forced	Treatment	15	.50	.07
	3-5 free	Sex, Track, Minority		.55	.05
Grades 3 & 4	1 forced	Total IQ 1	190	.63	.63
Total IQ 3	2 forced	Treatment	.5	.63	.00
	3-5 free	Track, Sex, Minority		.70	.07
Grades 5 & 6	1 forced	Total IQ 1	226	.72	.72
Total IQ 3	2 forced	Treatment	.0	.72	.00
	3-5 free	Track, Minority, Sex		.75	.03

TABLE 12

Results of Stepwise Regression Analyses for Grades One and Two

Criterion Variable: Total Raw Score on the Basic Posttest

Predictors: Pretest Raw Score, Treatment, Track, Sex,
Minority-Group Status, Grade, Age

Criterion	Step	Variable Entered	F to Enter	R^2	Increase in R^2
Total Raw Score on Basic Post-test	1 forced	Pretest raw score	136	.549	
	2 forced	Age	0	.549	.000
	3 forced	Treatment	9.3	.584	.035
	4-7 free	Sex, Track, Minority, Grade		.654	.070
	1 forced	Pretest raw score	136	.549	
	2-6 forced	Age, Grade, etc.		.617	.068
	7 forced	Treatment	11.2	.654	.037

same type of analysis was repeated for grades 1 and 2 using total raw scores with age and grade included (Table 12). All variables were forced to enter in the order shown; treatment was entered third in the first regression and was forced to enter last in the second regression. Note that using raw scores, the pretest predicts 55% of the variance in the posttest and all variables together predict 65% of the variance. The partial correlation of age with posttest after pretest has entered is negligible. Treatment predicts about 3 to 4% of the variance in posttest raw scores. Analysis of raw scores increases the predictable variance from 55% to 65% and decreases the apparent predictive importance of the treatment factor by about half.

Table 13 shows stepwise regression analyses for Verbal and Reasoning partscores with all grades combined. Predictor variables were IQ partscores on preceding tests, treatment, sex, and grade. (The two grade variables were dummy variables, one contrasting grades 1 and 2 with 3 and 4 and the other contrasting grades 3 and 4 with 5 and 6). Pretest IQ was forced into the equation first, and treatment second; the other variables were free to enter in any order. Our previous cautions about interpreting these analyses must be even more strongly emphasized here due to the high frequency of extreme scores in these IQ subscores. For all grades combined, treatment predicts a maximum of 2% of the variance in any IQ subscore. Inclusion of preceding subscores in addition to pretest increased the predictable variance by from 13 to 32%. For verbal IQ 54%, 70%, and 69% of the second, third, and fourth tests were predictable using all variables; for Reasoning IQ these figures were 35%, 46%, and 51% respectively, providing additional demonstration of the instability of the Reasoning subscores.

Investigation
of Treatment Effects
Using Analysis of Variance

RJ did not report fully on the analyses of variance performed and did not include any analysis of variance tables. Their only report on actual procedure used is contained in a footnote suggesting they were

. . . following the plan of a multifactorial analysis of variance with interest focused on the main effect of treatments, the two-way interactions of treatments by grades, treatments by tracks, treatments by sex, and treatments by minority-group status. Three-way interactions were also

TABLE 13

Results of Stepwise Regression Analyses

Using Separate Subscores

Criterion Variable: Separate Subscore IQ Posttests

Predictors: G1 (Grades 1-2 vs. 3-4), G2 (Grades 3-4 vs. 5-6),
Sex, Treatment, Preceding IQ Scores

Criterion	Step	Variable Entered	F to Enter	R^2	Increase in R^2
Verbal IQ 2	1 forced	VIQ 1	409.1	.53	
	2 forced	Treatment	.19	.53	.00
	3 free	Sex and Grade		.54	.01
Verbal IQ 3	1 forced	VIQ 1	427.9	.57	
	2 forced	Treatment	.6	.57	.00
	3 free	VIQ 2	132.2	.70	.13
	4-6 free	Grade and Sex		.70	.00
Verbal IQ 4	1 forced	VIQ 1	197.8	.48	
	2 forced	Treatment	4.1	.49	.01
	3 free	VIQ 3	72.4	.62	.13
	4 free	G2	34.2	.67	.05
	5 free	VIQ 2	10.3	.68	.01
	6-7 free	Sex and Grade		.69	.00
Reasoning IQ 2	1 forced	RIQ I	159.5	.30	
	2 forced	Treatment	5.7	.31	.01
	3-5 free	Grade and Sex		.35	.03
Reasoning IQ 3	1 forced	RIQ 1	106.5	.26	
	2 forced	Treatment	8.4	.28	.02
	3 free	RIQ 2	92.3	.44	.17
	4-6 free	Grade and Sex		.46	.02
Reasoning IQ 4	1 forced	RIQ 1	44.6	.18	
	2 forced	Treatment	.95	.18	.00
	3 free	RIQ 3	89.4	.43	.25
	4 free	RIQ 2	29.6	.51	.07
	5-7 free	Grade and Sex		.51	.01

computed for treatments by sex by tracks, treatments by sex by grade
levels, and treatments by minority-group status by sex. All other possible three-way and higher-order interactions yielded one or more
empty cells or a number of cells with *n*s so small as to weaken any
confidence in the results even though the analyses were possible in
principle.

All two-way and three-way analyses had unequal and nonproportional *n*s per cell, and Walker and Lev's (1953) approximate solution was employed. . . . The main effect of treatments was of course obtained in each of the analyses of variance, and *p*-values associated with the F's ranged from .05 to .002. (p. 94-95)†

The H.M. Walker and J. Lev approximate solution referred to by RJ is generally known as "unweighted means analysis." (See Appendix B.)

In this section, we discuss RJ's choice of computation method and their choice of factors to include in the analyses. Later in this section we report the results of several over-all analyses of variance as well as some analyses of variance within grade group. These serve primarily to demonstrate how widely the results of slightly different analytic procedures can vary when cell sizes are unequal and data have measurement and sampling problems.

Analysis of Variance in Unbalanced Designs

Application of analysis of variance to problems with unequal cell sizes although common has received too little attention in the literature beyond the cookbook details of computation. When cell sizes are unequal we are faced with several issues: The first and most important question concerns whether analysis of variance still is a valid procedure. Then, if so, what factors should be included? What computational method should be employed?

Standard analysis of variance procedures are based on the assumption that individuals have been assigned at random in equal numbers to each cell of the design (for factors like treatment) or selected at random from a larger group to fill each cell of a cross-classification with an equal number of individuals (for factors like sex). When all cell sizes are equal, the analysis of variance is said to be balanced or orthogonal and the estimates of the various main effects and interactions are orthogonal or statistically independent. If cell sizes in an AxBxC design are all equal, the sums of squares for main effects and interactions of factors A and B are unaffected by the inclusion or exclusion of factor C in the analysis. The only difference between an analysis of variance including only factors A and B and one including factor C also is the size of the error term; generally speaking, the more factors included in the analysis the smaller the error term. Under these circumstances, the full least squares solution with equal weights and the "unweighted means" procedure will produce identical analyses.

If cell sizes in a complete cross-classification were originally equal (or proportional) and subsequent subject losses were equally likely in each cell and thus final cell sizes are not related to the defining factors, an analysis of variance may be performed using the least squares procedure with an appropriate choice of weights (see Appendix B). Unweighted means analysis is "a quick approximate analysis to replace the tedious exact calculations" of least squares with equal weights (Scheffé, 1959, p. 362). The adequacy of approximation depends on ths amount of variation in cell sizes. With computers so readily available, there seems no justification for using unweighted means analysis. Consequently, we have used the least squares procedure exclusively in our reanalysis.

A major issue is the validity of the analysis of variance approach when cell sizes are related to ths defining factors or when collapsing over factors is necessary because cell sizes are zero or very small. Nonrandom cell fluctuations may occur when natural classifications such as intact classrooms are used or when differential subject loss occurs due to treatments. In these situations application of standard analysis of variance procedures may yield misleading results. We illustrate with two examples—one using natural classifications and one involving collapsing of categories. Both illustrate problems which occur in the RJ study.

A simple example based on the interaction in cell size between sex and track observed by RJ illustrates the misleading results an analysis of variance may yield when cell sizes are not independent of factors. Suppose boys and girls were distributed in the three ability tracks as shown in Table 14. Consider two different idealized situations which might produce this situation. In situation A, children are assigned to track strictly on the basis of ability; all children with IQs of 120 are placed in the fast track, all IQs of 100 are placed in the medium track, all IQs of 80 are placed in the slow track. Thus, to produce the cell sizes shown, the IQ distribution by sex must be that shown under situation A; the resulting cell means are also shown. In situation B, boys and girls have the same IQ distribution but girls are more likely to be placed in fast or medium tracks than boys. Thus not only are all the girls with IQs of 120 placed in hhe fast track, but also 20 of the girls with IQs of 100 are placed in the fast track, giving a cell mean for girls in the fast track of $(30 \times 120 + 20 \times 100)/50 = 112$. Conversely only 20 of the 30 boys with IQs of 120 are placed in the fast track, the rest are placed in the medium track and so on.

Applying the least squares procedure with equal weights we obtain a sizeable main effect for track in both situations. However, in situation A we would obtain no sex effect and no sex x track interaction. In situation B, we would obtain a sex effect and a track x sex interaction. Thus, in both situations an analysis of variance

TABLE 14

Example of Two Idealized Situations Producing an

Interaction in Sex x Track Cell Sizes

Number of Children

Track:		Fast	Medium	Slow	
Sex:	M	20	30	50	100
	F	50	30	20	100
		70	60	70	200

Situation A

Number of Children

IQ:		120	100	80
Sex:	M	20	30	50
	F	50	30	20

Mean IQ

Track:		Fast	Medium	Slow
Sex:	M	120	100	80
	F	120	100	80

Situation B

Number of Children

IQ:		120	100	80
Sex:	M	30	40	30
	F	30	40	30

Mean IQ

Track:		Fast	Medium	Slow
Sex:	M	120	106.7	88
	F	112	93.3	80

Actual Number of Children for Third and Fourth
Graders at Basic Posttest

Track:		Fast	Medium	Slow
Sex:	M	13	19	24
	F	30	16	13

TABLE 15

Idealized Example Showing the Effect of Dropping Factors

Number of Children

Track:		Fast	Medium	Slow
Treatment:	C	15	15	15
	E	5	1	5

Mean Gains

Track:		Fast	Medium	Slow
Treatment:	C	1.0	0.0	1.0
	E	1.0	0.0	1.0

produces misleading conclusions about IQ differences between the sexes.

Next we illustrate the misleading results that can be obtained when factors are dropped from an unbalanced design. In Table 15 is an idealized example of cell sizes for treatment x track in one grade—these figures are very similar to those actually obtained by RJ (see Table 2). Suppose that there is really no treatment effect but that children in the fast and slow tracks tend to gain more than children in the middle track and that we obtain the mean gains shown. When least squares with equal weights is applied to the treatment x track classification we obtain no treatment main effect and no treatment x track interaction. If the track factor were omitted because of small sample sizes, an analysis of variance would result in a spurious treatment effect due to the unbalanced sample sizes.

Although RJ assigned children to the experimental and control groups to produce cell sizes in the ratio of about 1 to 4, they used an unweighted analysis; every cell was assigned equal weights in the calculation of main effects and interactions. If there are no interactions, ths results are unaffected by the choice of weights and the standard procedure is to choose equal weights; see Appendix B for a more detailed discussion of this issue. If there is interaction, tests for main effects will be affected by the choice of weights. If the control group receives a weight of 4 and the treatment group a weight of 1 and all other effects are defined using equal weights, then the main effect for treatment and all interactions involving treatment will be the same as if equal weights were used; all other main effects and interactions will be affected by the choice of weights. Since there is no compelling reason to calculate sex and grade effects as if the experimental and control groups were equal in size, we decided to calculate most of the analyses of variance using a least squares analysis with proportional weights. The F tests for treatment and interactions with treatment will be the same with proportional weights as with equal weights but the calculated effects for sex, grade, and track will be much more heavily influenced by the larger control group using proportional weights. See Appendix B sections on *Least Squares* and *Proportional versus Equal Weights*.

Results of
Analyses of Variance

We computed several over-all analyses of variance using Total IQ pretest and Total IQ posttests as criterion variables. Two analyses of Total IQ gain scores were included for comparison with RJ's computations. Results are shown in Table 16. For completeness, the same analyses were computed for verbal and reasoning sub-scores, although interpretation of these results is doubtful (see Tables 17 and 18). Separate analyses of variance were computed within each grade group with posttest as criterion, gain scores as criterion, and posttest with pretest as a covariate (see Tables 20-22). The many analyses of variance reported allow us to compare the results obtained with different choices of factors, different criterion measures, different sets of weights, and different treatment of extreme scores.

Our discussion of analysis of variance in unbalanced designs illustrates how important the choice of factors is to the results obtained. Ideally treatment, track, grade, sex and minority group should all be included as factors in the analysis. This is impossible. Consequently some factors must be dropped or factors such as grade must be reduced from 6 levels to 3. Decisions about how to reduce the number of factors must be guided by the sampling and balancing needs of the design as well as by the purposes of the experiment.

We have dropped the minority group factor from our analyses of variance. The Mexican vs. non-Mexican factor was not a part of the design of the experiment; other variables describing ethnic origin or socioeconomic background could as easily have been analyzed. Since only 17% of the children were Mexican and this factor interacts with sex and track in cell size, its introduction sharply reduces cell sizes and it is unclear that a satisfactory assessment of its significance could be made.

Retaining grade, track, and sex there are still too few children per cell; there are 72 cells of which 6 are empty and many have only 1 or 2 children. As noted earlier, there are more girls in the high track and more boys in the low track so analyses of variance including both sex and track would likely produce misleading conclusions about the effects of these variables.

The children in grades 1 and 2 received TOGA Form K-2, those in grades 3 and 4 received Form 2-4, and those in grades 5 and 6 received Form 4-6. Since RJ combined these grades for some analyses, it seemed reasonable to use grade group rather than grade in some of our analyses to improve cell size.

Tables 16 through 18 summarize the results of analyses of variance with three choices of factors: treatment by grade group by sex (TxG'xS), treatment by grade by ability track (TxGxA), and treatment by grade group by sex by ability track (TxG'xSxA). Treatment by grade by ability track is the same as treatment by classroom and is probably the most important single analysis. For the basic posttest, grade 5 had to be deleted because classroom 5B did not take the Reasoning subtest. The other two analyses both contain treatment by grade group by sex and comparison of their

TABLE 16

Analysis-of-Variance Results: Total IQ

Effects Significant at .05 Listed

Criterion	Weights	Data Set	TxG'xS	TxGxA[††]	TxG'xSxA
				Factors	
Total IQ 1	E	All		G,A,GxA TxGxA	G,A
	P	All	G'		
	P	Truncated	G'		
Total IQ 2	P	All	T,G',S		
	P	Truncated	T,G'		
Total IQ 3	E	All	T	T,A,GxA	A,G'xSxA, TxG'xS
	P	All	T,G'		
	E	Truncated	TxG'xS		
	P	Truncated	G',TxG'xS		
Gain TIQ3-TIQ1	E	All		T,G	G',G'xA
Total IQ 4	P	All	S		
	P	Truncated	T,G'		

P = proportional weights
E = equal weights
TT = both pretest and posttest of interest truncated
A = denotes track or ability grouping
G' = the three grade levels--one and two, three and four, five and six
†† = Grade 5 has been deleted from this analysis because classroom 5-B did not take the Reasoning subtest

results shows what happens when the factor of ability track is included or excluded.

Analyses were performed on IQ scores from all four testings and on gain from pretest to basic posttest. Some analyses used all data, others truncated data; all were done using least squares, some using equal weights and some using proportional weights. Note that none of these analyses reproduce exactly any of those performed by RJ. Effects significant at the .05 level are indicated in

TABLE 17

Analysis-of-Variance Results: Verbal IQ

Effects Significant at .05 Listed

				Factors	
Criterion	Weights	Data Set	TxG'xS	TxGxA[††]	TxG'xSxA
Verbal IQ 1	E	All		A,GxA	A
	P	All	G',S		
	P	Truncated	*		
Verbal IQ 2	E	All	S		
	P	Truncated	S		
	P	TT	S		
Verbal IQ 3	E	All		A	A
	P	All	S		
	P	Truncated	*		
	P	TT	*		
Gain Verbal IQ 3- Verbal IQ 1	E	All		GxA	G'xA
Verbal IQ 4	P	All	G',S		
	P	Truncated	G',S		
	P	TT	G',S		

P = proportional weights
E = equal weights
TT = both pretest and posttest of interest truncated
A = denotes track or ability grouping
G' = the three grade levels--one and two, three and four, five and six
*There were no effects significant at .05
†† = Grade 5 has been deleted from this analysis because classroom 5-B
     did not take the Reasoning subtest

the tables; blank cells in the tables indicate analyses not performed.

Total IQ is the only measure sufficiently reliable to admit interpretation. Looking at the results for pretest Total IQ we gain a consistent picture of grade and ability track differences. Note, also, the triple interaction involving treatment. Results for Total IQ at

TABLE 18

Analysis-of-Variance Results: Reasoning IQ

Effects Significant at .05 Listed

			Factors		
Criterion	Weights	Data Set	TxG'xS	TxGxA[++]	TxG'xSxA
Reasoning IQ 1	E	All		G,A	G',A
	P	All	G',S		
	P	Truncated	G',S, G'xS		
Reasoning IQ 2	P	All	T,G'		
	P	Truncated	T,G'		
	P	TT	T,G'xS		
Reasoning IQ 3	E	All		T,A	G,A,TxG'xS TxG'xA G'xSxA
	P	All	T,G', G'xS		
	P	Truncated	G', G'xS		
	P	TT	G', G'xS		
Gain	E	All		G	G',TxS
Reasoning IQ 4	P	All	G'xS		
	P	Truncated	G'xS		
	P	TT	G'xS		

P = proportional weights

E = equal weights

TT = both pretest and posttest of interest truncated

A = denotes track or ability grouping

G' = the three grade levels--one and two, three and four, five and six

[++] = Grade 5 has been deleted from this analysis because classroom 5-B did not take the Reasoning subtest

second testing show how the presence of a sex effect is affected by the treatment of extreme scores.

Analyses of Total IQ basic posttest fairly consistently indicate some treatment effect although with the consistent superiority of the experimental group on the pretest these results can only be

TABLE 19

Analysis for Decrease in Error Variance Due to Use of Gain Scores

		Factors	
		TxGxA	TxG'xSxA
Total IQ	Error Variance Using Posttest	243	243
	Error Variance Using Gain	155	166
	Decrease in Variance	36%	32%
Verbal IQ	Error Variance Using Posttest	649	629
	Error Variance Using Gain	316	321
	Decrease in Variance	51%	49%
Reasoning IQ	Error Variance Using Posttest	584	627
	Error Variance Using Gain	610	714
	Decrease in Variance	-4%	-14%

regarded as suggestive that further more carefully chosen analyses should be undertaken. The fact that inclusion of more factors or exclusion of extreme scores reduces the treatment main effect to a three-way interaction is an indication that treatment effects are probably present in only a few cells of the classification.

The two analyses performed using gain scores with all the data and equal weights should provide results closest to those obtained by RJ. It is interesting to note that the only consistent results obtained in these two analyses are in grade effect. RJ may have obtained significant treatment effects in every analysis but we do not.

The consistent appearance of grade main effects and interactions involving grade confirms our earlier recommendation that separate analyses be made for different forms of TOGA (or grade groups).

Although we do not recommend analysis of verbal and reasoning partscores, we note that the analyses of the verbal sub-test provide no indication whatever of a treatment effect. Our analyses of reasoning gain do not confirm RJ's report of very significant main effects and the treatment effects which do appear for Reasoning IQ basic posttest disappear when extreme scores are removed.

Table 19 provides a summary of the relative precision of gain scores versus posttest scores obtained from analyses reported in

Table 16. These analyses were calculated using least squares with equal weights on all the data.

Turning now to separate analyses by grade group, Tables 20-22 provide comparisons of results obtained using pretest, gain scores, posttest only, and posttest with pretest as a covariate. Sex and track were not included in the analyses. Results are shown in terms of "expectancy advantage," that is, mean difference between experimental group and control group scores. Calculations were repeated on renormed and truncated IQ scores as well as raw scores for the first and second graders. (Pretest and posttest were jointly renormed or truncated.)

Examining Table 20 for Total IQ, we note that the three criterion measures and three sets of scores consistently show no expectancy advantage for third, fourth, fifth, and sixth graders. Results for first and second grades do seem to indicate an expectancy advantage but we note the 4- to 5-point advantage on the pretest and our earlier uncertainty that any of these analyses could be regarded as valid. These results warrant a closer look at first and second graders and further attempts to construct a valid analytic procedure in the face of pretest advantage, unreliability, and imbalance. Notice that renorming and truncation tend consistently to reduce apparent differences between the experimental and control groups.

Analyses of Verbal IQ and Reasoning IQ partscores are generally consistent with the results obtained for Total IQ. Note, however, how widely the apparent results differ depending on the treatment of extreme scores and the selection of criterion.

Analysis by Classroom

In our analyses to this point, we have treated the individual child as the experimental unit. What happens if the classroom is considered to be the unit of observation? Expectancy effects are after all probably group phenomena. The test information is provided to a teacher who in turn uses it on a whole classroom. Although eventually to be detected in individual student performance, expectancy effects may best be understood as a function of the particular groups in which they occur. There is, then, much justification for considering the experiment as a sample of 18 classrooms each with a subgroup of experimental and control subjects.

RJ applied the *t* test, the Wilcoxon, and the sign test to the eighteen pairs of mean gains. The number of children in the experimental and control groups vary widely from classroom to classroom and there are fairly sizeable IQ differences between

TABLE 20

Pretest to Basic Posttest "Advantage" in Total IQ

Mean scores for experimental group minus
mean scores for control group

	Pretest	Posttest	Gain	Posttest adjusted for pretest
Grade Group				
First and Second Grades				
All IQ	4.9	15.9*	11.0*	12.8*
Renormed IQ	4.5	13.7*	9.2*	10.8*
Truncated IQ	0.7	10.6*	9.9*	10.1*
Raw Scores	4.0	6.5*	2.5	4.4*
Third and Fourth Grades				
All IQ	0.5	2.3	1.8	2.0
Renormed IQ	0.5	2.1	1.6	1.6
Truncated IQ	-1.9	0.1	2.0	1.7
Fifth and Sixth Grades				
All IQ	4.3	4.5	0.2	-0.1
Renormed IQ	4.3	4.4	0.1	0.1
Truncated IQ	3.6	2.3	-1.3	-1.4

*Two-tailed $p < .05$

grades and between tracks. As a consequence, RJ's application of the *t* test is inappropriate, since its use requires that difference scores for each pair represent a random sample from *one* distribution.

Application of either the Wilcoxon signed ranks test or the sign test can be justified. A more serious problem, however, is that the gain scores are based on pre- and posttest results involving so many extreme scores. To illustrate the effect these extreme scores have on the results, we have performed the sign test and the Wilcoxon using the classroom means based on all the data and using classroom means recalculated on truncated data. That is, all individuals who had a score below 60 or above 160 on the relevant IQ measure were deleted from the sample. Pretest means were

TABLE 21

Pretest to Basic Posttest "Advantage" in Verbal IQ

Mean scores for experimental group minus
mean scores for control group

	Pretest	Posttest	Gain	Posttest adjusted for pretest
Grade Group				
First and Second Grades				
All IQ	0.4	10.5*	10.1*	10.2*
Renormed IQ	0.5	9.0*	8.5*	8.7*
Truncated IQ	-1.4	6.9	8.3*	7.8*
Third and Fourth Grades				
All IQ	4.0	-0.6	-4.6	-4.8
Renormed IQ	3.2	-3.6	-6.8*	-6.4*
Truncated IQ	-1.7	-7.3	-5.6	-5.9
Fifth and Sixth Grades				
All IQ	0.7	2.7	2.0	2.0
Renormed IQ	0.7	1.0	0.3	0.4
Truncated IQ	3.0	1.6	-1.4	-1.0

*Two-tailed $p < .05$

calculated only on those individuals present at the basic posttest. Classroom 5B had no posttest reasoning scores and was deleted where necessary.

Using all the data, the experimental group did not show significantly greater gains for Total IQ or Verbal IQ. The experimental group showed greater average gains in Reasoning IQ than the control group in 15 of 17 classrooms (two-tailed $p < .05$ for both the sign and the Wilcoxon tests). Looking at Tables 23 and 25 we see that for Reasoning IQ the experimental group had higher *pretest* means in 12 of 17 classrooms and that deletion of cases with extreme scores reduces the number of classrooms in which the experimental group gained more to 12 (not significant at $p < .05$ for either test).

TABLE 22

Pretest to Basic Posttest "Advantage" in Reasoning IQ

Mean scores for experimental group minus
mean scores for control group

	Pretest	Posttest	Gain	Posttest adjusted for pretest
Grade Group				
First and Second Grades				
All IQ	13.2	25.8*	12.6	21.0*
Renormed IQ	8.4	18.6*	10.2	13.7*
Truncated IQ	0.3	6.0	5.7	5.8
Third and Fourth Grades				
All IQ	-3.0	5.7	8.7	8.3
Renormed IQ	-3.0	6.3	9.3*	8.5*
Truncated IQ	-3.4	6.9	10.3*	9.0*
Fifth and Sixth Grades				
All IQ	4.0	8.9	4.8	5.4
Renormed IQ	4.1	3.9	-0.2	0.5
Truncated IQ	3.2	-1.6	-4.8	-4.0

*Two-tailed $p < .05$

A Closer Look at First and Second Graders

We have examined the results of many different analyses. For the third through sixth grade we conclude that there is no evidence of a treatment effect. Results for first and second graders, however, are inconclusive. Although the application of standard statistical procedures yields significant differences in treatments, the doubtful measurements and uncertain sampling procedure and balance make it unclear whether any of the analyses are valid. As a consequence we must take a closer look at total raw scores for these children. Using raw scores does not take differences in age into account but the stepwise regression reported in Table 12 in-

TABLE 23

Change in "Expectancy Advantage" by Classroom

Using All Data

Total IQ		Number of Classes		
	Posttest:	E > C	E < C	
Pretest:	E > C	8	1	9
	E < C	5	3	8
		13	4	17

Verbal IQ		Number of Classes		
	Posttest:	E > C	E < C	
Pretest:	E > C	8	3	11
	E < C	3	4	7
		11	7	18

Reasoning IQ		Number of Classes		
	Posttest:	E > C	E < C	
Pretest:	E > C	11	1	12
	E < C	2	3	5
		13	4	17

dicates that age is essentially unrelated to raw score gain for this group anyway. Table 26 shows the ages and pretest and posttest raw scores for first and second grade children grouped by sex and classroom. Control group children are listed according to rank on the pretest; each experimental group child is shown beside that control group child whose pretest score provides the closest match. (There are 95 control children and 19 experimental children.)

The attempt to find a comparable control group child of the same classroom and sex to match with each experimental group child reveals several things. First, there were four experimental children who could not be matched because there was no control

TABLE 24

Change in "Expectancy Advantage" by Classroom
with Extreme Cases Deleted

Total IQ   Number of Classes

		Posttest: E > C	E < C	
Pretest:	E > C	8	1	9
	E < C	5	3	8
		13	4	17

Verbal IQ   Number of Classes

		Posttest: E > C	E < C	
Pretest:	E > C	5	2	7
	E < C	4	6	10
		9	8	17 (1 tie)

Reasoning IQ   Number of Classes

		Posttest: E > C	E < C	
Pretest:	E > C	5	3	8
	E < C	4	4	8
		9	8	16 (1 E empty)

TABLE 25

Analysis of Mean Gains by Classroom

	Number of Classes E > C	Total Classes
All data		
Total IQ	11	17
Verbal IQ	12	18
Reasoning IQ	15[*][a]	17
Truncated data		
Total IQ	12[*]	17
Verbal IQ	9	17
Reasoning IQ	12	17

[*]Wilcoxon two-tailed p < .05
[a]sign test two-tailed p < .05

group child with a pretest score within ±3 points. Second, in the twelve cells there were two with no experimental child at all, 4 with one, 3 with two, and 3 with three children. Eleven of the experimental children were young in comparison with the control group, seven of these were the youngest in their group; four were old in comparison with their group, two being the oldest. Thus 16 of the 19 experimental group children were extreme in age in comparison with classmates of the same sex, and 9 were the most extreme.

Looking at pretest scores in the same way we find four experimental group children with low pretest scores, three with the lowest; seven experimental children with high pretest scores, three with the highest. Thus six of the experimental group children had pretest scores which were either the highest or the lowest among classmates of the same sex. We thus obtain somewhat clearer evidence that the control and experimental children do not provide closely comparable groups. It is therefore unclear whether any analysis can clarify the issue of whether or not there is a treatment effect. We may, however, gain some insight by looking further at the scores of the two groups.

First we examine raw score gains for the matched children (see Table 27). We note that reasonable matches were obtained only for 15 of the 19 experimental children. Looking at signs only we find $3 +$, $3 -$ for boys and $8 +$, $1 -$ for girls for a total of $11 +$, $4 -$. Using the sign test then there is no significant difference in gains between the pairs ($p > .05$ one sided). Using a Wilcoxon signed rank test, we obtain sum of negative ranks $= 24$ which is significant at .05. The median "excess gain" was 5. Since the magnitude of gain in raw score which is possible depends on the pretest score and thus varies considerably from grade 1 slow track to grade 2 high track, the t-test on gains does not seem a valid choice.

Looking at gain in relative rank for each experimental child in comparison with his classroom and sex group (e.g. for males in grade 1 track 1 the experimental child ranks lowest on the pretest but ranks eighth on the posttest for a change in rank of $+ 7$) we obtain two zero changes, four negative changes, and 13 positive changes. These results would be significant at the .05 level using the sign test. This analysis does not allow for the fact that individuals below the median on the pretest can be expected to have positive rank changes. Table 28 shows that 6 experimental children showed changes in rank from below to above the median and 1 showed a downward change; this is not significant.

Suppose we look at the problem a different way. If the treatment were effective we ought to be able to distinguish between experimental and control group children on the basis of posttest or

TABLE 26

Pre and Posttest Raw Scores for First and Second Graders

First Grade--Track 1

	Male						Female				
	Control		Experimental				Control		Experimental		
Age	Pre	Post	Age	Pre	Post	Age	Pre	Post	Age	Pre	Post
6.3	11	40	5.5	10	41.5*	6.2	7	26			
6.0	13	39				5.6	10	28	5.7	10	37
6.3	14	28				5.9	11	30			
6.0	15.	37				6.3	18	34			
5.6	16	53				6.0	20	31.5			
5.8	20	41.5				6.4	21	33			
5.8	21	26									
6.2	23.5	41.5									
5.6	27	35									
6.0	39	45									

First Grade--Track 2

Age	Pre	Post	Age	Pre	Post	Age	Pre	Post	Age	Pre	Post
6.0	5	44				5.7	22	31.5	5.7	19	44
5.8	9	37				6.2	22	27	5.7	20	52
5.8	15	31.5				6.3	23.5	41.5			
6.3	20	35				5.9	29	38			
5.6	21	41.5				5.8	35	43			
5.7	22	36				5.5	37	49			
5.7	23.5	45									
5.7	23.5	46									
5.6	27	49	5.5	26	43						
			6.0	41.5	56						

First Grade--Track 3

Age	Pre	Post	Age	Pre	Post	Age	Pre	Post	Age	Pre	Post
6.1	22	44				6.0	27	49			
5.5	23.5	44				6.2	27	39			
5.9	25	43				6.3	28	43			
6.0	31.5	53				5.7	29	52			
5.7	39	53				6.1	34	31.5	6.4	33	51
5.7	41.5	45				5.5	36	50			
6.4	41.5	55				6.2	38	38			
6.3	43	55									
6.2	44	48									
6.5	51	54									

*Sometimes two different raw scores corresponded to the same mental age; in converting IQ scores back to raw scores in these cases, the average of the two raw scores was used.

TABLE 26 (continued)

Second Grade--Track 1

	Male						Female				
	Control			Experimental			Control			Experimental	
Age	Pre	Post	Age	Pre	Post	Age	Pre	Post	Age	Pre	Post
7.2	17	41.5				7.2	22	26			
7.9	17	44				6.7	23.5	30			
			6.6	25	47	6.8	23.5	38			
6.7	31.5	37	7.5	31.5	48	7.2	25	45			
			8.1	31.5	48	6.9	26	39			
7.9	41.5	52				6.9	30	46			
						7.1	31.5	48			
						7.5	31.5	51			
						6.9	33	41.5			
						6.9	36	49			

Second Grade--Track 2

	Male						Female				
6.9	23.5	40				8.0	30	35			
6.7	26	46				7.1	31.5	51	6.8	33	43
7.2	26	41.5				7.1	49	57	7.0	46	59
7.0	31.5	53									
6.5	33	49									
7.3	33	51									
7.4	33	51									
6.9	35	49									
6.6	36	43									
7.3	41.5	44									
6.8	46	57	6.5	44	49						

Second Grade--Track 3

	Male						Female				
6.7	36	50				6.7	29	53			
6.7	40	55				7.3	40	40			
7.4	43	56				7.0	41.5	49			
7.5	46	55	6.9	46	57	7.0	41.5	51			
6.8	48	55				6.7	41.5	44	6.6	41.5	56
7.2	49	58				6.9	41.5	50			
6.5	50	57				7.2	43	50	7.4	45	56
7.1	50	58				6.8	47	47	6.8	45	59
7.4	50	56				7.4	53	55			
6.5	51	56	7.2	53	56						
			7.2	56	63						

TABLE 27

Excess of Gain by Experimental Children for the

15 "Matched" Pairs

		Sex	
		Male	Female
Grade 1			
Track	1	2.5	9
	2	-5.0, --	15.5, 27
	3	--	20.5
Grade 2			
Track	1	11, --, --	--
	2	-6	-9.5, 5
	3	2, -2, --	7.5*, 4, 14

*This experimental girl could have been matched with any of four control group children yielding "excess gains" of 12, 7, 6, 5; we have computed the average.

TABLE 28

Changes in Rank Within Sex and Classroom

		Posttest		
		Below median	Above median	
Pretest	Below median	2	6	8
	Above median	1	10	11
		3	16	19

gain scores. Can we do so? How successfully can children be classified as being from the experimental or control group on the basis of posttest or gain scores alone? For example, there is one experimental boy in grade 1, track 1; if we pick the boy with the highest posttest score from the eleven boys in grade 1, track 1, will it be the experimental child? Results using highest posttest scores are shown in Table 29 and using highest gain in Table 30.

Using highest posttest score, we correctly classify 10 of the 19 experimental children; using pretest we would identify 7; 5 are

TABLE 29

Children with Highest Post Score

| | No. of Children | | Children Selected | |
	from C*	from E†	Identity	Actually from E
Male				
Grade 1				
Track 1	10	1	C	0
2	9	2	C, E	1
3	10	0	--	--
Grade 2				
Track 1	4	3	C, E, E	2
2	11	1	C	0
3	10	3	C, C, E	1
Female				
Grade 1				
Track 1	6	1	E	1
2	6	2	C, E	1
3	7	1	C	0
Grade 2				
Track 1	10	0	--	--
2	3	2	C, E	1
3	9	3	E, E, E	3

| | | Children Actually | | |
		E	C	
Classified as	E	10	9	19
	C	9	86	95
		19	95	114

*C = Control Group
†E = Experimental Group

highest on both pre- and posttest. Using highest gain score we correctly classify 7 of the 19 experimental children. In either case, the expected number of experimental children correctly classified by selecting at random is 4.8 with a standard deviation of 1.65 (the expected number of boys correctly classified is 2.5 and of girls 2.3). Using gain scores then we do not correctly classify

TABLE 30

Children with Highest Gain Scores

	No. of Children from E[†]	Children Selected Identity	Actually from E
Male			
Grade 1			
Track 1	1	C*	0
2	2	C, C	0
3	0	--	--
Grade 2			
Track 1	3	E, C, C	1
2	1	C	0
3	3	C, C, C	0
Female			
Grade 1			
Track 1	1	E	1
2	2	E, E	2
3	1	C	0
Grade 2			
Track 1	0	--	--
2	2	E, C	1
3	3	E, E, C	2

Children Actually

		E	C	
Classified as	E	7	12	19
	C	12	83	95
		19	95	114

*C = Control Group
[†]E = Experimental Group

significantly more experimental children than we would expect to by selecting at random (see Appendix B).

Our closer look at first and second graders using raw scores to test for differences between experimental and control children has produced mixed results. The small sample size and lack of balance make it difficult to find a really appropriate analytic procedure.

There are indications that the control and experimental group children are insufficiently comparable to make any sound conclusions. Examination of the data suggests that there is no expectancy effect for boys but that there may be one for girls.

In conclusion then there is some evidence to suggest the presence of an expectancy effect in first and second graders. However, with so small and poorly balanced a sample, a conclusive analysis of these data is not possible. Definitive conclusions require additional experiments.

Appendix B:
Statistical Techniques

Analysis of Variance

Analysis of variance is a statistical technique designed to test the null hypothesis that the means of several groups are the same. A brief description of a standard two-way fixed effects analysis of variance with equal cell sizes will be used as an illustration. There are rc groups arranged in r rows and c columns; each group or cell contains the y scores of n individuals. For example, the c columns might be 2 treatments and the r rows might be 6 grades. Then we are interested in detecting differences between the means of the six grades, and interactions between treatments and grades.

To discuss the technique of analysis of variance it is helpful to write down a model for the individual scores, y_{ijk}, where i denotes rows, j denotes columns, and k denotes individuals within a group. It is assumed that the observations in a particular cell (row i, column j , for example) can be regarded as an independent random sample of n observations from a normal distribution with mean μ_{ij}

and variance σ^2 . The observations in different cells are also independent of each other. The variance is the same in each cell. This model can be written

$$y_{ijk} = \mu + \alpha_i + \beta_j + \gamma_{ij} + \varepsilon_{ijk}$$

where the ε_{ijk} are independently and normally distributed with mean zero and variance σ^2 . The effects, α_i , β_j , and γ_{ij} are defined so that $\sum_i \alpha_i = 0$, $\sum_j \beta_j = 0$, $\sum_i \gamma_{ij} = 0$, $\sum_j \gamma_{ij} = 0$. We then wish to test the three null hypotheses: H_0 : all $\alpha_i = 0$ or the means of the r rows are the same, H_0 : all $\beta_j = 0$ or the means of the c columns are the same, H_0 : all $\gamma_{ij} = 0$ or there are no differences in means between cells except those due to differences in row or column means.

The analysis of variance table is usually presented as follows:

Source	df	SS	MS
Rows	$r-1$	$cn\sum_i(\bar{y}_{i..}-\bar{y})^2$	$SS_R/(r-1)$
Columns	$c-1$	$rn\sum_j(\bar{y}_{.j.}-\bar{y})^2$	$SS_C/(c-1)$
Inter-action	$(r-1)(c-1)$	$n\sum_{ij}(\bar{y}_{ij.}-\bar{y}_{i..}-\bar{y}_{.j.}+\bar{y})^2$	$SS_I/(r-1)(c-1)$
Within cells	$rc(n-1)$	$\sum_{ijk}(y_{ijk}-\bar{y}_{ij.})^2$	$SS_{wc}/rc(n-1)$
Total	$rcn-1$	$\sum\sum\sum(y_{ijk}-\bar{y})^2$	

where $\bar{y}_{i..}$ denotes the mean of the observations in the ith row, $\bar{y}_{.j.}$ denotes the mean of the observations in the jth column, $\bar{y}_{ij.}$ denotes the mean of the observations in the i,j^{th} cell, and $\bar{y}$ denotes the mean of all the observations.

To carry out the tests, we note, for example, that under the null hypothesis of equal row means, MS_R/MS_{wc} has an F distribution with $r-1$ and $rc(n-1)$ degrees of freedom.

The null hypothesis of equal row means is rejected at the α level of significance if F for rows is greater than the $(1-\alpha)^{th}$ percentile of the F distribution with $r-1$ and $rc(n-1)$ degrees of freedom. (See for example Dixon and Massey, 1969, or Hays, 1963.)

This partition of the total sum of squares into mutually orthogonal (or independent) sums of squares due to each hypothesis is possible because the design is balanced (that is, the sample size in each cell is equal).

Least Squares Procedure for Analysis of Variance

The section on analysis of variance shows the general formulas for a two-way fixed effects analysis of variance with equal cell sizes. When cell sizes are unequal the formulas are not so simple to write down and the sums of squares for rows, columns, and interaction may not be orthogonal. To compute each particular analysis of variance we must fall back on the general principle underlying the derivation of the formulas, the least squares principle.

A model for a two-way classification where the levels of the first factor A are denoted by $i = 1, 2, \ldots, r$ and the levels of the second factor B denoted by $j = 1, 2, \ldots, c$ is

$$y_{ijk} = \mu + \alpha_i + \beta_j + \gamma_{ij} + \varepsilon_{ijk}$$

where there are n_{ij} observations in each cell and a total of N observations. The least squares principle states that the "best" estimates of μ, α_i, β_j, and γ_{ij} are those which minimize the sum of squared residuals about the line or those for which

$$\sum_i \sum_j \sum_k w_{ij} (y_{ijk} - \mu - \alpha_i - \beta_j - \gamma_{ij})^2$$

is minimized where the w_{ij} are some arbitrary system of

weights. Usually, equal weights, $w_{ij} = 1.0$, are cnosen
unless cell variances are known to be unequal.

To derive the estimators of μ, α_i, β_j, γ_{ij}, and the
sums of squares for the analysis of variance table, the
"normal equations" must be solved. A normal equation is
obtained for each parameter. For example, the normal equation
for μ is obtained by differentiating the expression for the
sum of squared residuals with respect to μ and setting the
result equal to zero. The normal equation for μ is

$$\sum_i \sum_j \sum_k y_{ijk} - N\mu - \sum_i \sum_j n_{ij}\alpha_i - \sum_i \sum_j n_{ij}\beta_j - \sum_i \sum_j n_{ij}\gamma_{ij} = 0 \ .$$

There are r equations obtained by differentiation with
respect to the α_i , c equations from the β_j , and rc
equations from the γ_{ij} .

The model for the cell means leads to $1 + r + c + rc$
equations, one for each parameter, but there are only rc
cell means, so only rc parameters can be estimated. To
obtain a unique solution, conditions must be imposed on the
parameters. The standard choice of conditions can be identified as follows. Select a set of weights $\{u_i\}$ corresponding
to the levels of A , where $u_i \geq 0$ and $\sum u_i = 1.0$. Select
a set of weights $\{v_j\}$ corresponding to the levels of B ,
such that $v_j \geq 0$ and $\sum v_j = 1.0$. Then impose conditions

$$\sum_i u_i \alpha_i = 0$$

$$\sum_j v_j \beta_j = 0$$

$$\sum_i u_i \gamma_{ij} = 0 \quad \text{all } j \ , \quad \sum_j v_j \gamma_{ij} = 0 \quad \text{all } i \ .$$

With these conditions, the mean of the ith level of A is
$A_i = \sum_j v_j \mu_{ij}$, the mean of the jth level of B is
$B_j = \sum_i u_i \mu_{ij}$, and we define $\mu = \sum \sum u_i v_j \mu_{ij}$, and
$\gamma_{ij} = \mu_{ij} - B_j - A_i + \mu \ .$

If, in fact, $\gamma_{ij} = 0$ for all i,j (no interaction), then the choice of weights $\{u_i, v_j\}$ will not affect SS_A or SS_B or any contrast among the α_i or β_j. Therefore, if there is no interaction, it will not matter what weights are chosen; the standard procedure would be to choose equal weights. If there is an interaction, the test of SS_{AB} is unaffected by the choice of weights but the main effects and tests on SS_A and SS_B will depend on the weights chosen. See the next section for an example showing the use of two different sets of weights.

If cell sizes do not differ widely and no other consider-ations suggest the use of unequal weights, the weights $\{u_i, v_j\}$ are usually chosen to be equal and the side conditions become

$$\sum_i \alpha_i = 0$$

$$\sum_j \beta_j = 0$$

$$\sum_i \gamma_{ij} = 0 \qquad \sum_j \gamma_{ij} = 0 \; .$$

If the n_{ij} are unequal, the normal equations will still be messy even if all the weights are chosen equal. However, if equal weights are used and all cell sizes are equal, the nor-mal equations become quite simple to solve. For instance, the first equation becomes

$$0 = \sum_{ijk} y_{ijk} - N\mu$$ and the formulas shown in the "Analysis of Variance" section hold.

For unequal cell sizes, the F test for the null hypothesis that all $\alpha_i = 0$ when the β_j and γ_{ij} are included in the model is

$$\frac{SS_A/[r-1]}{SS_E/[N-rc]}$$ where $SS_E = \sum_{ijk}(y_{ijk} - \hat{\mu} - \hat{\alpha}_i - \hat{\beta}_j - \hat{\gamma}_{ij})^2$

where the $\hat{\mu}_1$, $\hat{\alpha}_i$, $\hat{\beta}_j$, and $\hat{\gamma}_{ij}$ are obtained by solving the full set of normal equations and

$$SS_A + SS_E = \sum_{ijk} (y_{ijk} - \hat{\mu}^1 - \hat{\beta}_j^1 - \hat{\gamma}_{ij}^1)^2 \text{ where } \hat{\mu}^1, \hat{\beta}_j^1,$$

and $\hat{\gamma}_{ij}^1$ are obtained by solving the normal equations with all $\alpha_i = 0$. When the n_{ij} are all equal the estimators obtained under the two different conditions will be the same but when the n_{ij} are unequal $\hat{\mu} \neq \hat{\mu}^1$, etc.

For a full discussion, see H. Scheffé (1959). It should be noted that if there are any empty cells certain of the parameters will not be estimable.

Proportional versus Equal Weights

Refer to the discussion under "Least Squares Procedure for Analysis of Variance." An example will show what happens to the sums of squares for rows (A) and the sums of squares for columns (B) when the weights defining the side conditions are varied. Consider a 2x2 design with the cell sizes shown below.

$$n_{ij}$$

	B_1	B_2
A_1	10	2
A_2	10	2

Choose weights u and $1-u$ and v and $1-v$ to define the side conditions $u\alpha_1+(1-u)\alpha_2 = 0$ and $v\beta_1+(1-v)\beta_2 = 0$, $u\gamma_{1j}+(1-u)\gamma_{2j} = 0$, $v\gamma_{i1}+(1-v)\gamma_{i2} = 0$. Suppose the cell means are those shown below.

$$\bar{y}_{ij}$$

	B_1	B_2
A_1	1.0	2.2
A_2	1.0	1.0

Then the estimated mean for A_1 is $v(1.0)+(1-v)(2.2)$, for A_2 is 1.0, for B_1 is 1.0 and for B_2 is $u(2.2)+(1-u)(1.0)$. The standard choice of equal weights

$u = v = 1/2$ yields estimated means for A_1 and B_2 of 1.6 . However, since the cells for factor B_1 have five times as many cases it does not seem reasonable to give the cell means 1.0 and 2.2 equal weight in estimating the mean of A_1 . This suggests using weights $u = 1/2$ and $v = 5/6$, that is, weights which are proportional to the cell sizes, to obtain an estimated mean for A_1 of 1.2 . The use of equal weights yields sums of squares $SS_A = 1.20$ and $SS_B = 1.20$ while use of the proportional weights yields $SS_A = .24$ and $SS_B = 1.20$. Thus, in estimating the effect of A , the cell with a mean of 2.2 receives much less weight when its small sample size is taken into account by using proportional weights. The conclusions about B are unaffected by the use of proportional weights.

Unweighted Means Analysis

Unweighted means analysis is a quick approximate method of calculating an analysis of variance with unequal cell sizes. The only justification for its use is the labor involved in solving the normal equations by hand to obtain a least squares solution. The use of unweighted means analysis is not justified when the computer is available.

The computations for an unweighted means analysis can be performed using the formulas shown in the section "Analysis of Variance" except that $\bar{y}_{i..}$ and $\bar{y}_{.j.}$ are now replaced by $\bar{y}'_{i..} = \sum_j \bar{y}_{ij.}/c$ and $\bar{y}'_{.j.} = \sum_i \bar{y}_{ij.}/r$, n is replaced by $n_h = rc/\sum\sum n_{ij}^{-1}$, and the within-cells and total degrees of freedom are replaced by N-rc and N-1 respectively see (Winer, 1962). (A weighted means analysis could be calculated by analogy with a weighted least squares analysis.)

Simple Linear Regression

The technique of simple linear regression is based on

the model that

$$y_i = \mu + \beta(x_i - \bar{x}) + \varepsilon_i$$

where the ε_i are independent and normally distributed with mean zero and variance σ^2. The least squares estimators of μ and β are

$$\hat{\mu} = \bar{y}$$

$$\hat{\beta} = \frac{\sum(y_i - \bar{y})(x_i - \bar{x})}{\sum(x_i - \bar{x})^2} .$$

The model can arise in the situation when the x's are considered fixed and y is assumed to have a conditional normal distribution with mean $\mu + \beta(x_i - \bar{x})$ and variance σ^2, or in the situation where x and y are assumed to have a bivariate normal distribution.

A test of whether two independent regression lines are parallel or have the same slope β when the sample sizes n_1 and n_2 are equal and $\sigma_1^2 = \sigma_2^2$ is given by:

$$t = \frac{\hat{\beta}_1 - \hat{\beta}_2}{\frac{s_p}{\sqrt{n-1}}\sqrt{\frac{1}{s_{x_1}^2} + \frac{1}{s_{x_2}^2}}}$$

where $s_{x_i}^2 = \frac{\sum(x_{ij} - \bar{x}_i)^2}{n - 1}$ is the variance of the x's in sample i and

$$s_p^2 = \frac{s_{y_1 \cdot x}^2 + s_{y_2 \cdot x}^2}{2}$$

where $s_{y_1 \cdot x}^2 = (\frac{n-1}{n-2})(s_{y_i}^2 - \hat{\beta}_i^2 s_{x_i}^2)$.

The null hypothesis, $\beta_1 = \beta_2$, is rejected at level α if $|t| > t_{2(n-2), 1-\alpha/2}$, the $(1-\alpha/2)100\%$ point of the t distribution with $2(n-2)$ degrees of freedom. See, for example, Dixon and Massey (1969) for a more complete discussion and the modification of the formulas for $n_1 \neq n_2$.

Analysis of Covariance

     Analysis of covariance is an analysis of variance technique for situations in which information is available on a covariate x , such as a pretest or ability measure, which is strongly predictive of the y observations. Analysis of covariance is used to test the null hypothesis that the means of the y scores after "adjustment" using the x scores are the same in each group. The covariance procedure reduces possible bias in treatment comparisons due to differences in the covariate x and increases precision in the treatment comparisons by reducing variability in the y scores "due to" variability in the covariate x .

     The statistical model for a one-way analysis of covariance is composed of the four independent terms

$$y_{ij} = \mu + \alpha_i + \beta(x_{ij} - \overline{x}) + e_{ij} .$$

The e_{ij} are assumed to be an independent random sample from a normal distribution with mean zero and variance σ_e^2 . The basic difference between analysis of variance and analysis of covariance is that in an analysis of covariance the within-cell variation ε_{ij} is divided into two parts, variability predicted by a linear regression on x , and unexplained variability e_{ij} .

     The assumptions underlying the use of the analysis of covariance for testing the null hypothesis that there is no difference in group means for y not predictable from differences in group means for x (i.e., all $\alpha_j = 0$) are:

    a)   random assignment of individuals to groups,

    b) y scores have a linear regression on x scores within each group,

    c)   the slope of the regression line is the same for each group,

d)   for individuals in the same group with the same x
score, the y scores have a normal distribution,

e)   the variance of the y scores among individuals
with the same x score in the same group is the
same for all x scores and all groups,

f)   y scores can be represented by a linear combination
of independent -components: an overall mean, a group
effect, a linear regression on x , and an error
term.

For the details of the computations, see Dixon and Massey (1969)
For a discussion of the importance of the assumptions, see
J. D. Elashoff (1969).

Stepwise Regression

Stepwise linear regression is an ad hoc multiple linear
regression technique in which predictor variables are entered
one at a time into the equation in an attempt to obtain the
"best" set of predictors. The basic "forward selection"
procedure is as follows. At step one, the correlations between
the dependent variable y and each of the possible predictor
variables x_1, ..., x_p is computed. Then the x variable
with the highest correlation with y , call it $x_{(1)}$, is
"entered first" and the regression of y on $x_{(1)}$ is computed. At step two, the partial correlations are computed
between the remaining x variables and y , adjusted for
$x_{(1)}$. The variable, $x_{(2)}$, having the highest partial correlation with y is entered into the regression equation next.
At each subsequent step, the x variable which has the highest
partial correlation with y adjusted for the x's already in
the equation is entered. In other words then, at each step
the procedure enters the x variable which will produce the
greatest increase in the multiple correlation coefficient R .
The square of the multiple correlation coefficient, R^2 ,

gives the fraction of the variance of y which is "explained by" or predicted by the linear regression on the x variables in the equations.

This basic procedure called "forward selection" is modified in several ways in a standard stepwise regression program such as BMD 02R. At each step an F-statistic is calculated corresponding to each partial correlation. If the F-statistic for the x variable which has the highest partial correlation with y is less than a prespecified critical value of F, the procedure is terminated and no new variables are entered into the equation. In addition, at each step a check is made that each x variable in the equation still makes a significant contribution to R^2. An F-statistic is computed based on the partial correlation of x with y adjusted for the other x variables in the equation; if this F value falls below a prespecified F-to-remove value that x variable is deleted from the equation.

The BMD 02R program offers an additional option. Any of the x variables may be forced to enter the equation first irrespective of the value of their correlation with y. Additional x variables may be forced into the equation in a predetermined or partially predetermined order. That is, if two variables are designated to be forced in at level j, the variable with the highest partial correlation will be entered first and the other variable entered next; then the program proceeds to the next level of forced variables.

Leaving all the predictor variables "free," stepwise regression provides an ad hoc procedure for determining the relative importance of the x variables as predictors of y and for obtaining the "best" set of predictors. There is, of course, no guarantee that the variables selected will actually constitute the best set. Using the option of forcing variables in, a comparison may be made of the predictive power of a variable by itself versus its additional predictive power after other variables have been included.

Draper and Smith (1966) provide a useful introduction to multiple regression and stepwise regression.

Test Scores and Norms

The primary outcome of a test administration is an individual's raw score, usually the number of items in a test or subtest which were answered correctly. This number is useful for research purposes as it stands and should always be retained in whatever test performance records are kept. For many practical purposes, however, the raw score must be transformed in some way or related to other information to be interpreted properly.

Norms are tables of score distributions obtained in various reference groups. They relate raw score values to proposed conversion scores, like mental age, IQ, or grade equivalents. Most test manuals will provide norms at least for a "national" sample of people for whom the test is presumed appropriate. The best manuals, however, contain carefully specified breakdowns of norm tables showing distributions for sex, grade, geographic or social strata, or other subgroups of importance.

With norms and a standard error of measurement in hand, it is possible to interpret scores more completely. A child whose IQ score has changed 10 points in the past year may not be considered unusual if it is seen that 10 IQ points equals 4 raw score points at this part of the test range and the raw score standard error of measurement is 5 . For another child elsewhere in the range, a 10 point IQ change might be considered substantial. One cannot tell without knowing raw score equivalents and standard errors.

Published norms are often incomplete or have been extrapolated beyond the range of the distributions available in norm samples. Use of such extrapolations, whether computed by test maker or user, cannot be recommended. The central question in using any particular score or norm conversion is whether the obtained scale of measurement is meaningful for the particular population and interpretation intended.

Reliability

The reliability of a variable X, such as a score on an IQ test, is an estimate of the test's accuracy as a measuring instrument. Reliability can be defined in different ways depending on the model we choose to represent variation in obtained X scores. In practical situations it may be difficult to estimate reliability; many different formulas have been advanced, some based on correlations between equivalent forms of the test, some on measures of internal consistency of the test, and some on correlations showing the stability of the obtained score over repetitions of the test.

A standard model proposes that the observed score X is a combination of a true score x and an error e, that is

$$X = x + e$$

where x and e are independent and $\mu_e = 0$. Then the reliability of X is defined as the ratio of the true variance to observed variance, or the proportion of variance in X not due to error

$$R_x = \frac{\sigma_x^2}{\sigma_X^2} = \frac{\sigma_x^2}{\sigma_x^2 + \sigma_e^2}$$

Expected Number Correctly Classified

In a particular group there are n children, c of whom are in the control group, and t of whom are in the experimental group. Select t of the n children at random. What is the expected number of experimental children, e , among the t children selected? The number of experimental children among the t selected has a hypergeometric distribution with parameters n , t , c .

$$P(n_t = e) = \frac{\binom{t}{e} \binom{n-t}{t-e}}{\binom{n}{t}}$$

The mean of this distribution or the expected value of e is

$$E(e) = \frac{t^2}{n}$$

and

$$Var(e) = \frac{t^2 (n-t)^2}{n^2 (n-1)} \quad .$$

See, for example, Hays (1963).

Under the null hypothesis of no treatment effect, selection of the t children on the basis of posttest or gain scores should be equivalent to selection at random with respect to the two treatment groups. Therefore in group i , we expect to classify correctly t_i^2/n_i children by chance; since the groups are independent, the expected number correctly classified across all the groups is $\sum t_i^2/n_i$ and the variance is $\sum \dfrac{t_i^2 (n_i - t_i)^2}{n_i^2 (n_i - 1)}$.

Appendix C:
Pygmalion Reaffirmed

Robert Rosenthal and
Donald B. Rubin

1. *Overview: Pygmalion in the Classroom* Reaffirmed

In this paper, an invited response to the critique of Rosenthal and Jacobson (1968) (RJ) given in Elashoff and Snow (1970) (ES), we demonstrate that the ES document in *no* way impugns the validity of the RJ experiment.

A central thesis in ES is that there was a "wide variation in apparent results" when different methods of data analysis were employed, and that the statistically significant effects of teacher expectation reported by RJ were dependent upon the choice of a particular method of data analysis. This thesis is seriously in error. Indeed, as we shall show, the net effect of the varied statistical analyses carried out in ES is greatly to increase the cross-method generality of the results reported by RJ.

A second thesis in ES is that "imbalance" and "doubtful randomization" in the experimental and control groups invalidate the results of the RJ analyses. As we shall demonstrate, there is absolutely no reason to doubt the validity of the results of RJ.

Preparation of this paper was facilitated by a grant GS 29641X from the Division of Social Sciences of the National Science Foundation. We want to thank first Paul Holland and also Judy Koivumaki for their helpful suggestions on earlier drafts of this paper.

A third thesis in ES is that the RJ study is an isolated, unreplicated study. As will soon be clear, RJ is one of scores of studies indicating significant effects of interpersonal expectancy.

In addition, there are many other equally erroneous theses in ES to which we shall respond.

Before responding to ES in detail, we want to emphasize the basic simplicity of purpose and design of the RJ experiment. The intent was to study the effect of favorable teacher expectancy on pupil performance. The simplest experiment RJ might have done would have been to randomly assign some children to a condition of favorable teacher expectation and to retain the remaining children as controls. Because of the randomization, the average difference in posttest scores between the experimental and control group children would be an unbiased estimate of the effect of favorable teacher expectancy for the population for which the children are representative. In order to guide one's judgment as to whether the measured expectancy effect is real in the sense of replicable, some significance testing may often be desirable. To make such testing more powerful, that is, more able to detect real effects when they do, in fact, exist, we often try to control other sources of variation besides the treatment. Thus, the randomization in the RJ experiment was done within blocks of classrooms and a concomitant variable, the pretest, correlated with posttest, was recorded. Blocking and adjusting for individual differences on the pretest are procedures designed to increase the precision of the measurement of the expectancy effect or, equivalently, to increase the power of a test of the significance of the effect.

In what follows we shall demonstrate not only that the reanalyses in ES strongly support the conclusions of the RJ report but also that generally the criticisms offered in ES are unsound.

2. Additional Evidence for the Pygmalion Effect

It is consistently claimed in ES that wide differences in results arise when different dependent variables (posttest scores, gain scores, adjusted posttest scores) are employed and/or when the dependent variables are "transformed" (untransformed, renormed, truncated) and/or when various nonparametric methods are used. Despite the varied procedures employed in ES, the expectancy effects found in RJ remain undiminished.

Table 31 compares the RJ dependent variable (untransformed gain score) for total IQ with the eight other ES dependent variables for total IQ. (Unless further specified, references to IQ are to total IQ.) Within each grade level employed by ES, the RJ score and the 95% confidence interval for the RJ score are given along with the mean, median, lowest, and highest of the eight other scores. The means and medians of the ES scores agree remarkably well with the RJ scores. In addition, *all* ES scores fall well within the 95% confidence intervals for the RJ scores and thus are thoroughly consistent with them. In fact, the eight other ES scores are significant (two-tail, $p < .05$) if and only if the RJ score was significant (two-tail, $p < .05$) (note last column of Table 31). Clearly, then, these ES procedures reaffirm the validity of the RJ conclusions, and we are grateful to ES for the effort they expended in tabulating these additional dependent variables.

We are also grateful to ES for having redrawn one of the RJ figures, thereby suggesting our Figure 21. In their improvement over the RJ figure, ES tabulated the data noncumulatively and showed the proportion of children of grades one and two gaining varying amounts of IQ. However, they failed to note the statistical significance of the results they displayed. Based on ES' display of the data, Table 32 and Figure 21 show that there is a marked linear regression in the proportions (Snedecor and Cochran, 1967, pp. 246-247) of children who are experimentals on increasing levels of IQ gain ($p = .0012$, one-tail.) (Unless otherwise specified, all subsequent p values are one-tail.) Thus, while less than 8% of the children gaining less than 10 IQ points are in the experimental group, over 44% of the children gaining 30 or more IQ points are in the experimental group. Assuming no effects of teacher expectation we would expect about 17% of the children in either of these categories to be in the experimental group. Table 33 and Figure 22 show the same analysis for posttest scores. Not surprisingly, the results indicate a similar linear trend, which is equally significant.

Another analysis comparing the proportions of experimental and control group children showing high posttest or gain scores is even more elementary. We employed the concept suggested in ES that, since there are 19 experimental children in the first two grades, the topmost 19 gain scores or posttest scores should be earned disproportionately often by the children of the experimental group. Seven of the top 19 gain scores were earned by children of the experimental group, more than twice as many as we would expect to find by chance ($p < .02$). Table 34 shows the results of this analysis and the results of the same analysis performed on posttest scores. As it turned out, the results were identical and hence significantly supported the expectancy hypothesis.

The similar analysis performed in ES was done within sex and classroom. Note that the top 19 children chosen by the ES method are not necessarily the top 19 children of the entire sample of 114 children from the first two grades. Their analyses yield $p > .05$ for

Table 31

Comparison of Expectancy Advantage Scores in Total IQ

Employed in RJ vs Eight Others Employed in ES

Grade[a]	RJ	95% Confidence Interval for RJ[b]	All Eight Other ES Scores Mean	Median	Lowest	Highest	Total No. of Scores Sig. at $\dot{p} < .05$, two-tail (Maximum possible = 9)
1 and 2	11.0	(4.7, 17.3)	11.6	10.7	9.2	15.9	9
3 and 4	1.8	(- 3.8, 7.4)	1.7	1.8	0.1	2.3	0
5 and 6	0.2	(- 6.2, 6.6)	1.1	0.1	-1.4	4.5	0

[a] Categories employed in ES.

[b] Based on Mean square within = 164.24.

FIGURE 21.   PROPORTION OF CHILDREN WHO ARE EXPERIMENTALS GAINING
VARIOUS AMOUNTS OF TOTAL IQ

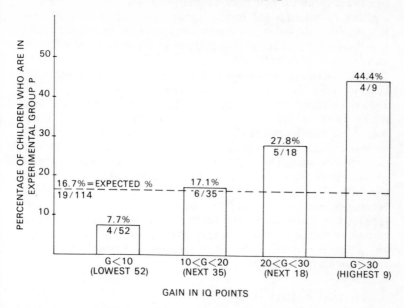

GAIN IN IQ POINTS

FIGURE 22. PROPORTION OF CHILDREN WHO ARE EXPERIMENTALS SHOWING
VARIOUS LEVELS OF TOTAL IQ POSTTEST SCORES

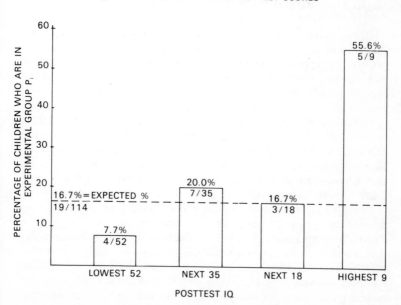

POSTTEST IQ

gain scores and $p < .001$ for posttest scores. ES reported the non-significant result of their peculiar method of analysis, but failed altogether to mention the highly significant result it also yielded. Regrettably this failure to report the results of significance tests that do not support the null hypothesis is not an isolated instance, as we shall now indicate.

In the discussion of the analysis by classrooms across all grades (ES tables 23, 24, and 25), six low power (Cohen, 1969, pp. 35, 155) significance tests were performed on posttest scores and gain scores. Of these six, two were specifically mentioned in ES and both were nonsignificant. Of the remaining four not specifically mentioned, three were significant at $p < .025$; and all six were in the predicted direction (Table 35). Similarly, when examining raw gain scores for matched children, ES give a Wilcoxon signed-ranks test with $p < .05$, two-tail, which was subsequently discarded because of some mysterious "dubious validity," while a less powerful sign test found to be "nonsignificant" ($p = .059$) was not discarded. A similar kind of sweeping-under-the-rug of "undesirably" low p values was shown in the evaluation of *Pygmalion* by A.R. Jensen in his famous paper (1969, p. 107).

3. Initial Equivalence of Experimental and Control Groups

In summarizing the results of the previous section we emphasize that they strongly support the hypothesis of the positive effects of positive interpersonal expectation. Indeed ES seem to be aware of this fact since they repeatedly instruct their readers not be believe the results of their own analyses because of "doubtful randomization" and "imbalance" in the experimental conditions.

Imbalance in sample size has nothing to do with randomization or the ability to obtain unbiased estimates of the effects of teacher expectation. To claim that unequal sample sizes hopelessly confound the analysis of an experiment (ES pp. 18, 76) is to claim that a comparison of the means of two random samples is confounded if the sample sizes are not equal; this claim is clearly false.

In addition, there is no way in which the idea of "doubtful randomization" can be employed to impugn the validity of the *Pygmalion* experiment. In the first place, as RJ clearly pointed out, the children of the experimental condition were assigned to that condition at random; specifically, RJ used the table of random numbers provided by H. Arkin and R.R. Colton (1950). In the second place, when the analyses that have been performed on post-

Table 32

Testing a Linear Regression of p_i on IQ Gain

Gain in IQ Points

Treatment	G < 10	10 < G < 20	20 < G < 30	G > 30	Total
Control (C)	48	29	13	5	95
Experimental (E)	4	6	5	4	19
Total (T)	52	35	18	9	114
p_i = E/T	.077	.171	.278	.444	.167

First order differences +.094   +.107   +.166

$\underline{b}$ = .112

$\underline{S}_b$ = .037

$\underline{Z}$ = 3.03

$\underline{p}$ = .0012, One-tail

Table 33

Testing a Linear Regression of p_i on IQ Posttest

Treatment	Lowest 52[a]	Next 35[a]	Next 18[a]	Highest 9[a]	Total
Control (C)	48	28	15	4	95
Experimental (E)	4	7	3	5	19
Total (T)	52	35	18	9	114
p_i = E/T	.077	.200	.167	.556	.167

First order differences +.123   -.033   +.389

$\underline{b}$ = .112

$\underline{S}_b$ = .037

$\underline{Z}$ = 3.03

$\underline{p}$ = .0012, One-tail

[a] Based on Ns given in ES Figure 2b.

Table 34

Children Earning 19 Highest Scores
(Grades 1 and 2)

	Post Scores	Gain Scores
% of 19 Experimental Children (P_e)	37%	37%
% of 95 Control Children (P_c)	13%	13%
Difference	24%	24%
χ^2	5.05	5.05
Z	+ 2.25	+ 2.25
one-tail p	.0122	.0122
h[a]	0.57	0.57
Approximate Magnitude, (Cohen, 1969)	Medium	Medium

[a] h is defined as $(2 \arcsin \sqrt{P_e}) - (2 \arcsin \sqrt{P_c})$

Table 35

Percentage of Classrooms Showing Expectancy Advantage

	Total N	Posttest		Gain	
		%	One-tail p	%	One-tail p
Total IQ	17	76%	.025[b]	65%	.166[a]
Verbal IQ	18	61%	.240[b]	67%	.119[a]
Reasoning IQ	17	76%	.025[b]	88%	.001[b]

[a] Reported in ES

[b] Not reported in ES

test and gain scores are performed on the pretest scores, they show no more difference between the experimental and control group children than would be expected by chance. Thus, for example, ES performed 36 over-all F tests of the significance of the difference between experimental and control group children on the pretest and obtained not a single F significant at $p < .05$ (ES Tables 16, 17, 18). If we consider all interactions of treatment condition with other variables as well as main effects of treatment we find that 192 (nonindependent) F tests of significance were made. Of these 192 F tests, only one, a triple interaction, was significant at $p < .05$, a result that could easily have occurred by chance, yet was singled out for comment in ES. Similarly, when ES analyzed pretest differences between experimental and control group children employing classrooms as the sampling unit, they found no significant differences (ES Tables 23, 24, and 25).

It may also be asked whether the linear regressions shown in Figures 21 and 22 and Tables 32 and 33 to be significant for IQ gain and IQ posttest might not also be significant for the pretest. Table 36 and Figure 23 show that this was not the case ($z < 1$).

Finally, employing the method of the "top 19" children introduced in ES, we can determine whether children of the experimental condition were overrepresented among the children earning the highest 19 scores on the total IQ pretest. Under the hypothesis of successful randomization we expect to find about three or four children of the experimental group among the top 19. What we find is just what we would expect under conditions of successful randomization: four of the top 19 were members of the experimental group ($x^2 = 0.05$, $df = 1$, $p = .82$).

In summary, since children were assigned to the experimental condition by means of a table of random numbers and since, furthermore, dozens of tests on the distribution of the pretest gave no indication that there had been any failure of randomization, it becomes most difficult to understand the continued concern shown in ES over "doubtful randomization." It must be concluded that ES' basis for not believing the effectiveness of randomization remains obscure and that the validity of the RJ experimental design has been thoroughly confirmed.

4. Misleading Citation of Replication Research in ES

As mentioned earlier, the purpose of all the tests of significance performed is basically to evaluate the "reality" of the expectancy effect obtained, i.e., to determine its replicability under virtually

Table 36

Testing a Linear Regression of p_i on Pretest IQ

Treatment	Pretest Levels of IQ				
	Lowest 52[a]	Next 35[a]	Next 18[a]	Highest 9[a]	Total
Control (C)	44	31	13	7	95
Experimental (E)	8	4	5	2	19
Total (T)	52	35	18	9	114
p_i = E/T	.154	.114	.278	.222	.167
First order differences		-.040	+.164	-.156	

$\underline{b}$ = .035

$\underline{S}_b$ = .037

$\underline{z}$ = 0.95

$\underline{p}$ = .1711

[a] Based on Ns given in ES' Figure 2b.

Table 37

Percentage of Studies Reaching Given $\underline{p}$ Levels

	Type of Study		
Significance Level	Teachers (N=37)	Experimenters (N=162)	Total (N=199)
$\underline{p} \leq$ .05 (one-tail)			
% in Predicted Direction	38%	33%	34%
% in Unpredicted Direction	0%	4^+%	4^-%
% Not Significant	62%	63%	63%
$\underline{p} \leq$ .01 (one-tail)			
% in Predicted Direction	14%	14%	14%
% in Unpredicted Direction	0%	1%	1%
% Not Significant	86%	85%	85%
$\underline{p} \leq$ .001 (one-tail)			
% in Predicted Direction	11%	9%	10%
% in Unpredicted Direction	0%	0%	0%
% Not Significant	89%	91%	90%

FIGURE 23. PROPORTION OF CHILDREN WHO ARE EXPERIMENTALS SHOWING VARIOUS LEVELS OF TOTAL IQ PRETEST SCORES

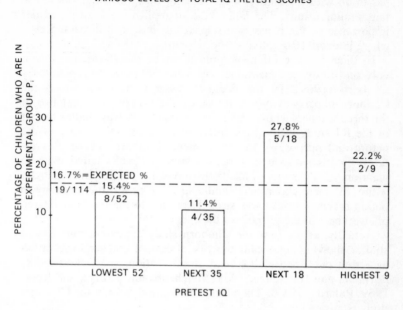

FIGURE 24. EFFECTS OF TEACHER EXPECTATION IN SIX GRADES

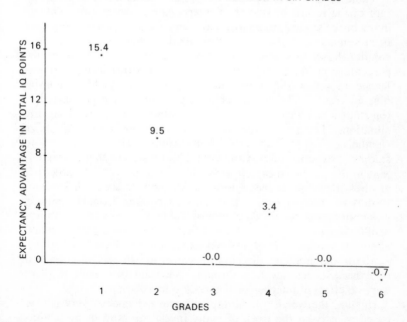

identical conditions. There is another sense of replicability which has to do with the ability of the same or other investigators to obtain similar results. The latter kind of replication is of particular importance to the behavioral sciences as has been discussed elsewhere in detail (Rosenthal, 1966, 1969b).

In their brief mention of replications of the *Pygmalion* effect, only one study was mentioned by name, a failure to replicate by Claiborn (1969). In the doctoral dissertation upon which the Claiborn paper was based, it was candidly explained that two of the three teachers whose experimental condition was similar to that of the RJ study were either fully aware or partially aware of the nature and purpose of the experiment (Claiborn, 1968). Regrettably, in his subsequent article, Claiborn (1969) failed even to mention this difficulty in his discussion of his results. Interestingly, within his three classrooms similar to those in RJ, the tendency to obtain reversed results was strongly related to the teachers' degree of awareness of the purpose of the experiment.

Actually, at the time the Claiborn study appeared, numbers of studies showing significant positive effects of teacher expectation had been published and/or read at conventions (e.g., Beez 1968; Burnham and Hartsough, 1968; Meichenbaum, Bowers, and Ross, 1969; Palardy, 1969). Therefore, the citation of only the Claiborn study is misleading.

Table 37 has been provided to give the reader an up-to-date picture of the results of studies of interpersonal expectation. Though many of the studies summarized are very recent, most of them have been summarized elsewhere (Rosenthal, 1969b, 1971). The first column shows for studies of teacher and counselor expectations the percentage yielding results at the .05, .01, and .001 levels of significance in either direction and the percentage yielding nonsignificant results. The second column gives the corresponding data for studies conducted in laboratories rather than in everyday life situations. The percentages of studies reaching various levels of significance agree remarkably well, from studies of teachers to studies of experimenters. Considering those studies that are significant in the predicted direction vs. those that are not, all three x^2s are less than one. It seems reasonable, then, to see both kinds of studies of interpersonal expectation as coming from a common population, and the third column of Table 37 shows the combined results. If there were no expectancy effect, we would expect to find about 10 studies of interpersonal expectation to have reached a $p < .05$ in the predicted direction; however, 67 studies have reached or exceeded that level, a virtually unobtainable result if there were no effect of interpersonal expectation.

In sum, the weight of the replicational evidence is very heavy, based as it is on the work of many investigators in many laboratories throughout the country. Although no experimental results in the behavioral sciences can be expected to show $p < .05$ in every study or even every other study, the ability of the effects of interpersonal expectancy to be demonstrated over a wide variety of dependent variables, investigators, laboratories, states, and even countries suggests a robustness not common to the ephemeral phenomena of the behavioral sciences. The *Pygmalion* effect is real.

5. Other Criticisms

Before going on to consider other criticisms in ES, we summarize very briefly what has been reported to this point:
1) The *Pygmalion* effect does *not* depend upon the particular method of data analysis employed. This fact is clear using the evidence provided in ES.
2) The experiment was fully randomized and there is *no* reason to doubt the initial equivalence of the experimental and control groups. This fact is clear using the evidence provided by approximately 200 tests performed in ES.
3) *Pygmalion* is *not* an isolated study of interpersonal expectation. This fact is clear based upon results of scores of studies including many dealing specifically with teacher expectations.

In addition to the criticisms refuted above, there are other unsound criticisms of *Pygmalion* put forward in ES.
1) *ES imply that RJ should have employed stepwise regression in their analysis of a fully randomized experiment.* At best, when all the appropriate interactions are entered, stepwise regression will give the same results as an analysis of variance. More usually, interactions and nonlinear trends are not entered, in which case stepwise regression eliminates important estimates and displays, and usually inflates the residual variance. In addition, stepwise regression inclines the user to assess the importance of a phenomenon using only the percentage of variance explained and to ignore not only the expected difference between means but even the direction of the effect (e.g. see ES Tables 11, 12, and 13).
2) *ES imply that RJ should have employed a rigid null hypothesis decision procedure.* An ES imperative is to interpret no relation unless $p < .05$ and to report p values less than .01 as $< .01$. The wisdom of this null hypothesis decision approach has been called into serious question not only by psychologists (Rosenthal, 1968; Rozeboom, 1960) but by a number of eminent statisticians as well. R. A. Fisher, for example, showed little patience with advice of the sort offered in ES, i.e., handy

hints as to how and when to accept or reject hypotheses (Cochran, 1967). Fisher preferred to keep track of whatever *p* value was obtained and to wait and see what happened in subsequent observations. Finally, we find the ES orientation toward *p* values thoroughly inconsistent with the mental set they recommend, namely that of a detective rather than that of an attorney.

3) *ES imply that RJ's claim to increasing effects of teacher expectation in going from higher to lower grades is untenable.* However, the RJ data showed a significant interaction of treatment with linear regression of grades ($t = -2.69$, $df = 308$, $p < .01$, two-tail; Snedecor and Cochran, 1967, p. 278). In order to indicate the magnitude of this linear trend in average differences, we give the Pearson *r* between grade level and mean expectancy advantage per grade: $r = -.86$. (RJ, p. 74) One display of this trend is shown in Table 38 and another in Figure 24. These results indicate that there is a clear and significant increasing effect of teacher expectation as one moves from higher to lower grades.

4) *ES imply that RJ should have employed the various ES data transformations.* However, these transformations are statistically biased. Using the interval of 60-160, ES renormed by setting scores outside the range equal to the endpoints and truncated by discarding children outside the range. These would not have been biased procedures if they had been carried out only on pretest scores, even though they might restrict the generalizeability of the resultant analyses. On the other hand, when these procedures are applied to posttest scores they are biased and tend to diminish any real differences between the experimental and control groups. Specifically, if the experimental condition tends to increase or decrease scores, the above procedures would tend to distort or discard experimental scores more often than control scores thus making the means of the experimental and control groups more similar. For example, if one discarded all subjects whose posttests did not equal 100, the experimentals and controls would not differ on posttest.

5) *ES imply that RJ obtained effects that were trivial in magnitude even though they may have been significant statistically.* In their discussion of the effects of teacher expectation on reading grades, ES point out that none of the differences in gains between experimental and control groups is as large as one full grade point equivalent (e.g., the difference between a grade of B and C). Since the standard deviation of the pretest reading grades was less than unity, ES appear to require an effect size to be larger than a standard deviation in order for it to be regarded as important. Such requirements, exceeding consider-

Table 38

Expectancy Advantage in Total IQ Gain After One Year

Grade	IQ Points	S.D. Units[a]	One-tail $\underline{p} < .05$	Approximate Magnitude (based on Cohen, 1969)
1	+ 15.4	+ .83	.002	large
2	+ 9.5	+ .51	.02	medium
3	- 0.0	- .00	--	zero
4	+ 3.4	+ .18	--	small
5	- 0.0	- .00	--	zero
6	- 0.7	- .04	--	tiny (and reversed)
Total	+ 3.8	+ .21	.02	small

[a] σ = 18.48 based on pretest total IQ of all available children, N = 382.

Table 39

Expectancy Advantage in Reading Score Gain After One Year

Grade	Reading Scores	S.D. Units[a]	One-tail $\underline{p} < .05$	Approximate Magnitude (based on Cohen, 1969)
1	+ .55	+ .56	.03	medium
2	+ .48	+ .48	.05	medium
3	+ .42	+ .42	.04	medium
4	+ .07	+ .07	--	very small
5	- .02	- .02	--	tiny (and reversed)
6	+ .08	+ .08	--	very small
Total	+ .17	+ .17	.05	small

[a] σ = 0.99 based on pretest reading scores of all available children, N = 313.

ably a reasonable definition of even a large effect size (Cohen, 1969, p. 24), are very questionable. The actual effect sizes for reading scores are shown to be at least medium size in three of the six grades (Table 39). Note also the similarity of effect sizes between the expectancy advantages in reading score gains (Table 39) and total IQ gains (Table 38); the correlation between these two measures over the six grade levels is +.74. (RJ, p. 100)

6) *ES imply that the RJ dependent variables are unsuitable measures of intellectual performance.* We find in ES a concern over the "low" reliability ($r = .74$, Column 1, RJ Table A-30) of TOGA along with the implication that this threatens the validity of the *Pygmalion* experiment. Actually, unreliability (increased noise) can never account for the significant results of a fully randomized experiment; rather it can serve only to reduce power. We find also in ES the argument that the correlation of .65 between TOGA and subsequent ability track placement given in Rosenthal (1969a) does not adequately demonstrate validity. That correlation is higher than the correlation between scores on the nonverbal section of the Lorge-Thorndike and scores on the very same test retaken after an intervening summer. Finally, correlations between TOGA and other tests of intellectual performance are even higher (e.g., TOGA with Lorge-Thorndike: $r = .73$). Another recommendation found in ES is to employ raw scores as the dependent variable instead of IQ. We prefer to use IQ scores since it is IQs, not raw scores, that are used in the real world to make decisions.

7) *ES imply that RJ was insufficiently reviewed prior to publication.* We feel, on the contrary, that RJ was unusually thoroughly reviewed prior to publication. In addition to having prior journal publication, the RJ research was solicited and approved for inclusion in a volume prepared for Division 9 of the American Psychological Association, *Social Class, Race, and Psychological Development* (Holt, Rinehart and Winston, 1968), edited by Martin Deutsch, Irwin Katz, and Arthur Jensen. Numerous other scholars in the behavioral sciences have requested permission to reprint the RJ research in their own volumes of readings, both before and after RJ was published. In addition, the award committee of Division 13 of the American Psychological Association presented the first prize of the Cattell Fund Award to the RJ research in 1967.

Given space, we could continue to refute criticisms of RJ and indicate many other errors in ES, but we feel that our point has been made.

Conclusions

We now conclude this response to the criticisms of *Pygmalion* (RJ) given in Elashoff and Snow (1970) (ES), having demonstrated the following:

1) The results of the varied ES analyses are absolutely consistent with the results of the RJ analyses and indicate a significant effect of teacher expectations.

2) RJ was a completely randomized experiment and the numerous ES tests of the success of the randomization give absolutely no reason to doubt the pre-experimental equivalence of the experimental and control groups and thus no reason to doubt the validity of the conclusions above.

3) Positive effects of favorable interpersonal expectations have been obtained in numerous experiments conducted by dozens of researchers and thus the result in RJ can in no sense be considered a fluke.

4) Although there were among the ES criticisms a few useful notions which we employed in this reply, in the main the numerous criticisms advanced in ES were neither sound nor constructive.

Appendix D:
Pygmalion Rebutted

Janet D. Elashoff
and Richard E. Snow

1. Introduction

Rosenthal and Rubin (1971) (RR) have attempted to reaffirm the validity of the Pygmalion experiment of Rosenthal and Jacobson (1968) (RJ). Their responses to our critique and reanalysis are rebutted point for point below.

2. RR's Additional Evidence

RR conclude that our reanalyses only confirm the original RJ finding. They provide two tables showing results for all grades. Table 31 summarizes nine analyses showing "significant" expectancy effects in grades 1 and 2 and no "significant" expectancy effects in grades 3 to 6. It is heartening that RR now admit no effects beyond the first two grades, since the text of RJ's report implied generally significant results. However, in Table 35 at the end of the section they return to an over-all analysis by classroom in which they claim that we suppress a number of interesting *one-tail p* values. Our final version does mark the corresponding *two-tail p* values which are less than .05 for mean gain and no longer refers to the Wilcoxon having dubious validity. It is surprising to note, however, that RR have omitted from Table 35 the corresponding table and *p* values for the pretest (see table below). Note that these results for Verbal and Reasoning IQ are almost identical with posttest results.

Percentage of Classrooms Showing Expectancy Advantage

	Pretest		
	Total N	%	One-tail p
Total IQ	17	53%	.50
Verbal IQ	18	61%	.24
Reasoning IQ	17	70%	.07

The other three tables and two figures in the section are concerned only with grade 1 and 2 children. As we clearly noted, a number of analyses of the grade 1 and 2 children showed "significant" results but we were doubtful of the validity of these results for reasons which RR continue to ignore. These doubts, occasioned by the problems of extreme scores, doubtful randomization, imbalance, are restated below.

RR Figures 21 and 22 and Tables 32 and 33 simply rehash the same data, still using arbitrary subdivisions of doubtful gain scores. Our redrawing of RJ figures was meant to correct misleading charts, not to sanction the data or analyses on which they were based. RR's analyses of the top 19 children, reported in Table 34, ignore variables of sex and classroom and are therefore subject to possible confounding effects.

3. Initial Equivalence of Experimental and Control Groups

Using a table of random numbers per se does not ensure proper randomization. It is still not clear in just what grouping or blocking RJ randomized or how they ensured that the number of experimental boys (or girls) per classroom assigned to the experimental group was between 40 and 60% of the experimental group children in that classroom. In their reply RR say only that "randomization in the RJ experiment was done within blocks of classrooms." (RR, p. 2) The form of analysis *must* reflect the way in which randomization was carried out. Their statement that "dozens of tests on the distribution of the pretest gave no indication that there had been any failure of randomization" (RR, p. 6) does not reassure us. To be certain that randomization is adequate one must know the details of the assignment procedure. Tests of significance on pretest scores would detect only gross failures of randomization. Indeed, the pretest classroom results reported above and the fact that Grade 1 and 2 experimental children have total scores averaging 4.9 IQ points higher, and reasoning scores averaging 13.2 IQ points higher than the control group does cast doubt on the effects of randomization. These average differences are sizeable differences; due to the excessively high variability in pretest scores for these children, they are not statistically significant at the 5% level. However, using a one-tail test, as RR routinely do, the Reasoning difference reaches $p <$ .10. RR's Table 36 and Figure 23 also exhibit the generally higher pretest scores.

RR's argument that imbalance in sample size can not confound an analysis confuses two important issues. First, it is well known that the true significance level of a test comparing the means of two random samples *can* be affected by inequality of sample sizes when the variances are not equal (see our discussion on page 38.) Secondly, the experimental and control groups in the RJ experiment are *not* two random samples; randomization was apparently performed within sexes and within "blocks of classrooms." If imbalance in sample size is sufficient to keep these factors out of the analysis, any effects related to these factors may become confounded with the treatment effect.

Clearly then, the unclear randomization procedure, initial advantage of the experimental group, and imbalance in cell sizes, do cast serious doubt on RJ's results.

4. Replication Attempts

RR criticize as misleading our isolated citation of Claiborn's (1969) failure to replicate the *Pygmalion* effect, and list four other studies showing significant positive effects. It is interesting to note that none of the four studies RR cite includes IQ as criterion and several differ fundamentally in design from the RJ study. Yet they are apparently offered as examples of replication. Our reference was offered as an example of improved research design; it was not intended as a summary of literature. A clearer and more comprehensive picture of replication attempts and related studies is provided by Philip Baker and Janet Crist's chapter. In the Baker and Crist summary table, it can be seen that of nine studies (other than RJ) attempting to demonstrate teacher expectancy effects on IQ, none has succeeded. Of twelve expectancy studies including pupil achievement measures as criteria, six have succeeded. Of seven studies including measures of observable pupil behavior, three have succeeded. And of seventeen studies including measures of observable teacher behavior, fourteen have succeeded. Thus it seems that teacher expectancy effects are most likely to influence proximal variables (those "closest" in a psychological sense to the source of effect, e.g., teacher behavior) and progressively less likely to influence distal variables (or variables psychologically remote from the source of expectations). IQ, the most remote of pupil variables, is unlikely to be affected. These results are consistent with a Brunswikian view of teacher-learner interaction (Snow, 1968). They suggest that teacher expectancies may be important and are certainly deserving of study, but they fail utterly to support *Pygmalion's* celebrated effect on IQ.

Summarizing a collection of studies is always a treacherous undertaking. No study is ever truly a replicate of another. Many basic differences between studies are glossed over in generalizing and the temptation is strong to turn such lists of results into "box scores" or percentages of studies for and against some conclusion, as in RR's Table 37. Such tables have little value as literature summaries. Instead, literature reviewers should look for subcategories or patterns of findings that make some kind of psychological sense, such as the rough continuum of dependent variables noted above. Such patterns will likely reveal more about the psychology of the phenomena at hand than will blind sweeping-together and totalling of findings.

5. RR's "Other Criticisms"

We reproduce, and subsequently reject, each of RR's seven specific points below.

1) *ES imply that RJ should have employed stepwise regression in their analysis of a fully randomized experiment.* We did not imply that RJ should have used stepwise regression but stated that they should have examined the magnitude of the treatment effect. To quote from our section on stepwise regression: "Our only purpose is to gain an impression of the relative importance of any treatment effect." (ES, p. 97)

2) *ES imply that RJ should have employed a rigid null hypothesis decision procedure.* We emphasized that reporting of p values is no substitute for plotting and probing of the basic raw data or for examining the practical significance of results. We did not advocate a rigid decision procedure; we urge researchers to "Report p values within *any* predetermined limits, but *interpret* no relation unless p is less than a fixed value such as .05."(ES,

p. 45, emphasis added here) RR's description of R. A. Fisher's approach is perfectly consistent with our emphasis. Keeping track of all findings while research continues is good science; building theory on marginal findings is not.

3) *ES imply that RJ's claim to increasing effects of teacher expectation in going from higher to lower grades is untenable.* If the effects were significant in grades 1 and 2, and were not significant in grades 3, 4, 5, and 6, then to describe this dichotomy as showing ". . . increasing expectancy advantage as we go from the sixth to the first grade . . ."(RJ, p. 74) implies that there are some positive effects in the middle and higher grades as well. This gives the reader a false impression.

4) *ES imply that RJ should have employed the various ES data transformations.* We did not imply that RJ should have used particular transformations, but that they should have questioned the extreme scores obtained and dealt with them in some manner. To quote from our section on renorming and truncation:

"Neither procedure is wholly adequate since the effect on various statistical approaches is unknown, but analyzing the data in all three ways, in original IQ form, in truncated IQ form, and in renormed IQ form provides information on the sensitivity of the results to the presence of extreme scores."(ES, p. 85)

5) *ES imply that RJ obtained effects that were trivial in magnitude even though they may have been significant statistically.* The point was that, of eleven school subjects, only one, reading gain, showed "significant" expectancy advantage at the 10% level. Our exact statement was: "The choice of scale makes the gains and differences in gains look large when, in fact, most are considerably less than one grade point." (ES, p. 15) Our Figure 23 and RR's Table 39 show that, of the 12 (6 grades by 2 groups) mean gain scores, all but 2 were less than three-tenths of a grade-point and of the six differences in gains, three were less than one-tenth of a grade point.

6) *ES imply that the RJ dependent variables are unsuitable measures of intellectual performance.* The "reliability" (stability over one year) of TOGA Reasoning IQ scores is $r_c = .45$ and $r_e = .50$ in grades 1 and 2. Such values are usually considered low. However, our main concern stemmed from the many instances of extreme IQ scores and the apparent instability of these scores across the four testings. Unreliability does cast doubt on the *meaning* of results. As to validity, a correlation of .65 between TOGA and subsequent track placement is a correlation calculated among *three* means. To quote our earlier statement: "A test could predict a gross, three-level judg-

ment of academic status well and still be nearly useless as a measure of *individual* intellectual ability or growth."(ES, p. 39, emphasis added here) The essential evidence regarding validity in this situation would have been for RJ to include another independent measure of IQ in their study to show that it too displayed expectancy effects.

7) *ES imply that RJ was insufficiently reviewed prior to publication.* RR's list of the RJ publications, reprintings, and award, notwithstanding, we retain our view that *Pygmalion* was inadequately and prematurely reported to the general public.

6. Criticisms Ignored by RR

Among the important criticisms of RJ not dealt with by RR, a few should be briefly noted here and one deserves special emphasis. We stated that the RJ report is misleading, that it includes technical inaccuracies, and that it omits important information. Readers should review the relevant sections of our report to satisfy themselves on these points.

We also stated that the RJ report ignores the psychological meaning of the scores on which it rests. Perhaps this is the most basic problem with *Pygmalion*. The point was made by R. L. Thorndike (1968, 1969), and by Snow (1969), and recurs regularly in our reanalysis as well as in these final remarks, but it is not mentioned by RR. What, after all, does an IQ of zero, or 17, or 31, or 202, or 210 really mean? What does an IQ gain of 100, 125, or 135 really mean? Our scatterplots of pre- and posttest scores for grades 1 and 2 (Figures 11, 12, and 13) show clearly that the apparent large expectancy effects are due to the influence of unusually high or low scores on the regression lines. Are these extreme points RJ's "magic" children? What is the magic? Are we really dealing with the effects of self-fulfilling prophecy on the intellectual growth of imbeciles and geniuses, operating through teachers who do not even remember the names of the individuals they have supposedly influenced so profoundly? Or are we dealing with misunderstood test instructions? Or uncontrolled test administration? Or selective teacher coaching? Or teacher encouragement for guessing? Or chance? Or what?

With an IQ scale of questionable meaning, we advocated a return to raw scores as the lesser of two evils. For data analysis in research, the scores and scales that are most likely to lead to valid interpretation should be used. RR rejected our preference for raw scores because, they say, IQ is used for decision making in the real world. But decisions in the real world must also assume a meaningful scale of measurement. Fortunately for RJ, no school decisions were made on the basis of *Pygmalion* IQ's," or their study might have lost about 35% of its grade 1 and 2 children to special education programs.

RR conclude that our reanalysis ". . . in *no* way impugns the validity of the RJ experiment" and that ". . . there is absolutely no reason to doubt the validity of the results of RJ."(RR, p. 1) We can only reiterate the hope that researchers will play detective rather than attorney in their pursuit of knowledge relevant to social problems. In view of the readiness with which the public uncritically accepts results like those of the *Pygmalion* study, and of the importance and complexity of phenomena like "teacher expectancy" and "intellectual growth," investigators *must* doubt; they must be critical of their own work. Absolute certitude ill behooves research.

References

Substantive References

Anderson, D. F. and Rosenthal, R., "Some effects of interpersonal expectancy and social interaction on institutionalized retarded children," *Proceedings of the 76th Annual Convention of the American Psychological Association* 3 (1968): 479-480.

Beez, W. V., "Influence of biased psychological reports on teacher behavior and pupil performance," *Learning in Social Settings*, eds. M. W. Miles and W. W. Charters, Jr., Boston: Allyn and Bacon, Inc., 1970.

Brophy, J. and Good, T. L., "Teachers' communication of differential expectations for children's classroom performance: Some behavioral data," *Journal of Educational Psychology* 61 (1970): 365-374.

Brown, W. E., "The influence of student information on the formulation of teacher expectancy," *Dissertation Abstracts* 30 (1970): 4822-A.

Cahen, L. S., "An Experimental Manipulation of the Halo Effect." Doctoral dissertation, Stanford University, 1966.

Claiborn, W. L., "Expectancy effects in the classroom: A failure to replicate," *Journal of Educational Psychology* 60 (1969): 377-383.

Conn, L.; Edwards, C.; Rosenthal, R.; and Crowne, D., "Emotion perception and response to teacher expectancy in elementary school children," *Psychological Reports* 22 (1968): 27-34.

Evans, J. T. and Rosenthal, R., "Interpersonal self-fulfilling prophecies: Further extrapolation from the laboratory to the classroom." *Proceedings of the 77th Annual Convention of the American Psychological Association* 4(Part 1) (1969): 371-372.

Fleming, E. S. and Anttonen, R. G., "Teacher expectancy, or my fair lady," *American Educational Research Journal* 8 (1971 a): 241-252.

————, "Teacher expectancy as related to the intellectual, academic, and personal growth of primary age children," *Monographs of the Society for Research in Child Development* (1971 b), in press.

Flowers, C. E., "Effects of an arbitrary accelerated group placement on the tested academic achievement of educationally disadvantaged students," *Dissertation Abstracts* 27 (1966): 991-A.

Freedman, A. L.; Carlsmith, J. M.; and Sears, D. O., *Social Psychology.* Englewood Cliffs, N. J.: Prentice-Hall, Inc., 1970.

Gephart, W. J. and Antonopolos, D. P., "The effects of expectancy and other research-biasing factors," *Phi Delta Kappan* 50 (1969): 579-583.

Goldsmith, J. S. and Fry, E., "The test of a high expectancy prediction on reading achievement and IQ of students in grade 10 (or, Pygmalion in puberty)," submitted to *American Educational Research Journal,* 1970.

Good, T. L., "Which pupils do teachers call on?" *The Elementary School Journal* 70 (1970): 190-198.

Guskin, A. E. and Guskin, S. L., *A Social Psychology of Education.* Reading, Mass.: Addison-Wesley Publishing Company, Inc., 1970.

Haberman, M., "The relationship of bogus expectations to success in student teaching," *The Journal of Teacher Education* 21 (1970): 69-72.

Hastorf, A. H.; Schneider, D. J.; and Polefka, J., *Person Perception.* Reading, Mass.: Addison-Wesley Publishing Company, Inc., 1970.

Heider, F., *The Psychology of Interpersonal Relations.* New York: John Wiley & Sons, Inc., 1958.

Jacobs, J. F., "Teacher expectancies: Their effect on peer acceptance." Paper presented at Annual Meeting, American Educational Research Association, Minneapolis, 1970.

José, J., "Teacher-pupil interaction as it relates to attempted changes in teacher expectancy of academic ability and achievement," *American Educational Research Journal* 8 (1971): 39-49.

Kester, S., "The communication of teacher expectations and their effects on the achievement and attitude of secondary school students," *American Educational Research Journal,* 1971 (in press).

Meichenbaum, D. H.; Bowers, K. S.; and Ross, R. R., "A behavioral analysis of teacher expectancy effect," *Journal of Personality and Social Psychology* 13 (1969): 306-316.

Palardy, J. M., "What teachers believe, what children achieve," *Elementary School Journal* 69 (1969): 370-374.

Pitt, C. C. V., "An experimental study of the effects of teachers' knowledge or incorrect knowledge of pupil I.Q.'s on teachers' attitudes and practices and pupils' attitudes and achievement," *Dissertation Abstracts* 16 (1956): 2387-2388.

Rist, R. C., "Student social class and teacher expectations: The self-fulfilling prophecy in ghetto education," *Harvard Educational Review* 40 (1970): 411-451.

Rosenthal, R., *Experimenter Effects in Behavioral Research.* New York: Appleton-Century-Crofts, 1966.

———, "Self-fulfilling prophecy," *Psychology Today* 2 (1968 a): 44-51.

———, "Self-fulfilling prophecies in behavioral research and everyday life," *Claremont Reading Conference Thirty-Second Yearbook*, 1968(b), ed. M. P. Douglass, 16-33.

———, "Interpersonal expectations: Effects of the experimenter's hypothesis," *Artifact in Behavioral Research*, eds. R. Rosenthal and R. Rosnow. New York: Academic Press, Inc., 1969 (a).

———, "Teacher expectation and pupil learning." Paper prepared for a conference on The Unstudied Curriculum sponsored by the Association for Supervision and Curriculum Development. Washington, D. C., January 8-11, 1969 (b). Also in Overly, N. V., ed., *The Unstudied Curriculum*. Washington, D. C.: Association for Supervision and Curriculum Development, 1970 (a).

———, "Empirical vs. decreed validation of clocks and tests," *American Educational Research Journal* 6 (1969 c): 689-691.

———, "Another view of Pygmalion," *Contemporary Psychology* 15 (1970 b): 524.

Rosenthal, R. and Jacobson, L., "Teacher's expectancies: Determinants of pupils' IQ gains," *Psychological Reports* 19 (1966): 115-118.

———, "Teacher expectations for the disadvantaged," *Scientific American* 218 (1968 a): 19-23.

†———, *Pygmalion in the Classroom: Teacher Expectation and Pupils' Intellectual Development.* Copyright © 1968 by Holt, Rinehart and Winston, Inc., New York. Portions reprinted by permission of Holt, Rinehart and Winston, Inc. (b)

———, "Self-fulfilling prophecies in the classroom: Teachers' expectations as unintended determinants of pupils' intellectual competence," *Social Class, Race, and Psychological Development*, eds. M. Deutsch; I. Katz; and A. Jensen. New York: Holt, Rinehart and Winston, Inc., 1968 (c).

Rothbart, M.; Dalfen, S.; and Barrett, R., "Effects of teacher's expectancy on student-teacher interaction," *Journal of Educational Psychology* 62 (1971): 49-54.

Rubovits, P. and Maehr, M., Pygmalion analyzed toward an explanation of the Rosenthal-Jacobson findings. Paper presented at Annual Meeting, American Educational Research Association, Minneapolis, 1970.

Schrank, W. R., "The labeling effect of ability grouping," *The Journal of Educational Research* 62 (1968): 51-52.

———, "Further study of the labeling effects of ability grouping," *The Journal of Educational Research*, 63 (1970): 358-360.

Seaver, W. B., "Effects of Naturally Induced Teacher Expectancies on the Academic Performance of Pupils in Primary Grades." Doctoral dissertation, University of Illinois, 1971.

Secord P. F. and Backman, C. W., *Social Psychology*. New York: McGraw-Hill, Inc., 1964.

Simon, W. E., "Expectancy effects in the scoring of vocabulary items: A study of scorer bias," *Journal of Educational Measurement* 6 (1969): 159-164.

Snow, R. E., "Brunswikian Approaches to Research on Teaching," *American Educational Research Journal* 5 (1968): 475-489.

Tagiuri, R., "Person perception," *The Handbook of Social Psychology, Vol. III: The Individual in a Social Context*, eds. G. Lindzey and E. Aronson. Reading, Mass.: Addison-Wesley Publishing Company, Inc., 1969.

Tagiuri, R. and Petrullo, L., eds., *Person Perception and Interpersonal Behavior*. Stanford, Calif.: Stanford University Press, 1958.

Willis, B. J., "The influence of teacher expectation on teachers' classroom interaction with selected children." *Dissertation Abstracts,* 30 (1970): 5072-A.

Methodological References

Cochran, W. G., "Errors of measurement in statistics," *Technometrics* 10 (1968): 637-666.

Cronbach, L. J. and Furby, L, "How should we measure change—or should we?" *Psychological Bulletin* 74 (1970): 68-80.

Dixon, W. J. and Massey, F. J., *Introduction to Statistical Analysis*. 3rd. ed. New York: McGraw-Hill, Inc., 1969,

Draper, N. R. and Smith, H., *Applied Regression Analysis*. New York: John Wiley & Sons, Inc., 1966.

Elashoff, J. D., "Analysis of covariance: A delicate instrument," *American Educational Research Journal* 6 (1969): 383-402.

————, "A model for quadratic outliers in linear regression," submitted to *Journal of the American Statistical Association*, 1970.

Elashoff, R. M., "Effects of errors in statistical assumptions," *International Encyclopedia of the Social Sciences* 5 (1968): 132-142.

Hays, W. L., *Statistics for Psychologists*. New York: Holt, Rinehart and Winston, Inc., 1963.

Huff, D., *How to Lie with Statistics*. New York: W. W. Norton & Company, Inc., 1954.

Scheffé, H., *The Analysis of Variance*. New York: John Wiley & Sons, Inc., 1959.

Tukey, J. W., "Analyzing data: Sanctification or detective work?" *American Psychologist* 24 (1969): 83-91.

Walker, H. M. and Lev, J., *Statistical Inference*. New York: Holt, Rinehart and Winston, Inc., 1953.

Reviews

Aiken, L., "Review of *Pygmalion in the Classroom*," *Educational and Psychological Measurement* 29 (1969): 226-228.

Barber, T. X. and Silver, M. J., "Fact, fiction, and the experimenter bias effect," *Psychological Bulletin Monographs* 70 (6, Part 2) (1968): 1-29.

Coles, R., "What can you expect?" *The New Yorker,* 9 April (1969), pp. 169-177.

Doob, L., "Review of *Pygmalion in the Classroom*," *The Key Reporter*, Spring 1969.

Hutchins, R., "Success in schools," *San Francisco Chronicle*, 11 August 1968.

Kohl, H., "Review of *Pygmalion in the Classroom*," *The New York Review of Books*, 12 September 1968, P. 31.

McCurdy, J., "Testing of IQs in L.A. primary grades banned," *Los Angeles Times*, 31 January 1969.

Roberts, W., "Voices in the classroom," *Saturday Review*, 19 October 1968, P. 72.

Snow, R. E., "Unfinished Pygmalion," *Contemporary Psychology* 14 (1969): 197-200.

Thorndike, R. L., "Review of *Pygmalion in the Classroom*," *American Educational Research Journal* 5 (1968): 708-711.

————, "But you have to know how to tell time," *American Educational Research Journal* 6 (1969): 692.

Time, 20 September 1968, p. 62.

References to Appendix C

Arkin, H., and Colton, R. R., *Tables for statisticians.* New York: Barnes & Noble, Inc., 1950.

Beez, W. V., "Influence of biased psychological reports on teacher behavior and pupil performance." *Proceedings of the 76th Annual Convention of the American Psychological Association* (1968): 605-606.

Burnham, J. R. and Hartsough, D. M., "Effect of experimenter's expectancies ("The Rosenthal effect") on children's ability to learn to swim." Paper presented at the meeting of the Midwestern Psychological Association, Chicago, May, 1968.

Claiborn, W. L., "An investigation of the relationship between teacher expectancy, teacher behavior and pupil performance." Doctoral dissertation, Syracuse University, 1968.

———, "Expectancy effects in the classroom: a failure to replicate," *Journal of Educational Psychology* 60 (1969): 377-383.

Cochran, W. G., "Footnote to an appreciation of R. A. Fisher," *Science* 156 (1967): 1460-1462.

Cohen, J., *Statistical Power Analysis for the Behavioral Sciences.* New York: Academic Press, Inc., 1969.

Elashoff, J. D. and Snow, R. E., "A case study in statistical inference: Reconsideration of the Rosenthal-Jacobson data on teacher expectancy." Technical Report No. 15, Stanford Center for Research and Development in Teaching, School of Education, Stanford University, December, 1970.

Jensen, A. R., "How much can we boost IQ and scholastic achievement?" *Harvard Educational Review* 39 (1969): 1-123.

Meichenbaum, D. H.; Bowers, K. S.; and Ross, R. R., "A behavioral analysis of teacher expectancy effect," *Journal of Personality and Social Psychology* 13 (1969): 306-316.

Palardy, J. M., "What teachers believe—What children achieve," *Elementary School Journal* 69 (1969): 370-374.

Rosenthal, R., "Experimenter expectancy and the reassuring nature of the null hypothesis decision procedure," *Psychological Bulletin Monograph Supplement* 70 (1968): 30-47.

———, "Empirical vs. decreed validation of clocks and tests," *American Educational Research Journal* 6 (1969a): 689-691.

———, "Interpersonal expectations: Effects of the experimenter's hypothesis," *Artifact in Behavioral Research*, eds. R. Rosenthal and R. L. Rosnow, New York: Academic Press, 1969b, pp. 181-277.

———, "Teacher expectation and pupil learning," *Teachers and the learning process*, ed. R. D. Strom, Englewood Cliffs, New Jersey: Prentice-Hall, 1971, pp. 33-60.

Rosenthal, R. and Jacobson, L., *Pygmalion in the Classroom.* New York: Holt, Rinehart and Winston, Inc., 1968.

Rosenthal, R. and R. L. Rosnow, eds., *Artifact in Behavioral Research.* New York: Academic Press, Inc., 1969.

Rozeboom, W. W., "The fallacy of the null-hypothesis significance test." *Psychological Bulletin* 57 (1960): 416-428.

Snedecor, G. W. and Cochran, W. G., *Statistical methods.* 6th ed. Ames, Iowa: Iowa State University Press, 1967.

Charles A. Jones Publishing Company
698 High Street   Village Green
Worthington, Ohio   43085

61 J 6